ESOTERIC RELIGIOUS STUDIES SERIES

Book#17

ANCIENT EGYPTIAN
Rituals and Symbolism

Esoteric Religious Studies Series
ANCIENT EGYPTIAN
RITUALS AND SYMBOLISM

Author: Diohka Aesden
Publisher: Cineris Multifacet
Publication Date: 2024
ISBN: - 9798882626401

For inquiries and permissions, please contact:
Cineris Multifacet
mythmaster@mythological.center

Design and Typesetting:
Cineris Multifacet

Cover Design:
Cineris Multifacet

Disclaimer:

Manufactured in the United States of America

First Edition: 2024

ISBN-13: - 9798882626401

19   54   95

This page left intentionally blank.

OTHER BOOKS IN THIS SERIES

A WORLD OF ESOTERIC THOUGHT

ANCIENT EGYPTIAN
RITUALS AND SYMBOLISM

To Jan Assmann -

This book is especially dedicated to **Jan Assmann**, an absolutely essential Egyptologist and scholar of comparative religion.

Jan's **"normative inversion"** terminology became a very intriguing concept within the study of the relationship between Egyptian religion and Judaism.

Jan Assmann passed away shortly before the publication of this book, 19 February 2024.

May his memory remain alive, as this and many other books could not have existed without his work.

To **Eternal Life**,

- Diohka

Committed to
the 7

and to
Pope Philo III

A

ALPHA

May the reader of the **Esoteric Religious Studies Series** be blessed abundantly. We extend our heartfelt gratitude for your engagement with this sagacious study of esoteric traditions. As you adventure through the pages, may your mind be illuminated with knowledge and your heart be filled with *wisdom*. May the insights and revelations within these texts expand your understanding and bring clarity to your spiritual path. May you be well-informed, enriched, and guided by the sacred *wisdom* that unfolds before you. May this series be a source of encouragement, transformation, and blessings upon your life.

If you enjoy the words of this book, please consider leaving a review in the marketplace you found it so that its content can reach even more interested individuals.

Please visit the author page of Diohka Aesden to keep up with new releases on religion, esoterica, mythology, and other related topics.

TABLE OF CONTENTS
A

Ω

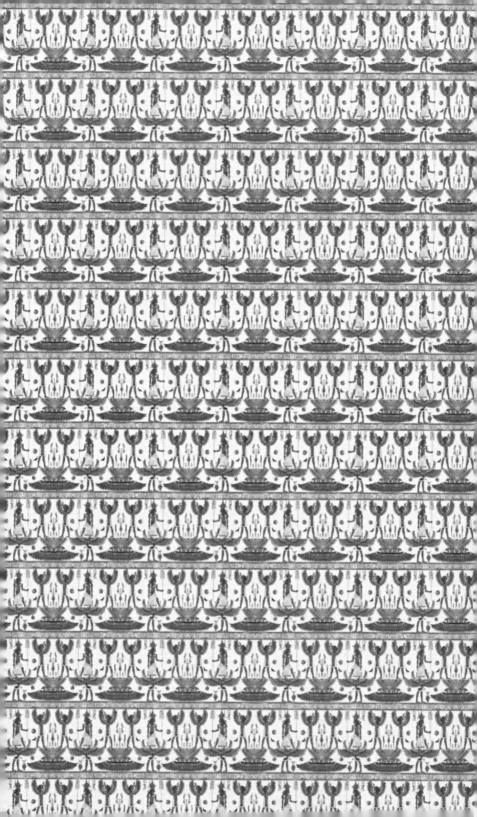

INTRODUCTION

The study of ancient Egyptian rituals and symbolism occupies a necessary place in esoteric religious studies, offering profound insights into one of humanity's oldest and most enigmatic spiritual traditions. This civilization, which flourished along the banks of the Nile for thousands of years, developed an opulent atlas of religious beliefs and practices that continue to fascinate scholars, practitioners, and seekers of mystical knowledge. The Egyptians' intricate cosmology, elaborate rituals, and profound symbolism speak to universal themes of life, death, and the afterlife, embodying a quest for understanding that transcends cultural and temporal bounds. At the heart of ancient Egyptian religion was the concept of Ma'at, the universal principle of truth, balance, and order, which governed all aspects of existence, all the way from the movements of the stars to the seasonal flooding of the Nile, and the moral conduct of individuals. The maintenance of Ma'at through rituals, offerings, and personal virtue was central to Egyptian religious practice, reflecting a worldview in which the human, natural, and divine worlds were intimately connected. This holistic approach to religion, which integrated myth, ritual, and ethics, offers valuable perspectives for esoteric studies, highlighting the interdependence of the physical and spiritual, and the place of humanity's agency in sustaining the universal order.

Egyptian rituals, opulent in symbolic actions and offerings, were designed to engage the gods, secure their favor, and ensure the wellness of the community and the natural world. These rituals ranged from daily temple worship and personal devotions to elaborate festival celebrations and funerary rites, each imbued with deep symbolic meaning. The use of symbolism in Egyptian rituals—whether through the language of hieroglyphs, the iconography of gods and goddesses, or the ritual use of objects like amulets and scepters—conveys complex theological concepts in a visual and material form, making the sacred accessible and comprehensible.

The symbolism of Egyptian art and architecture further illustrates the civilization's religious and cosmological beliefs. Temples, pyramids, and tombs were not just architectural marvels but also sacred spaces designed to reflect universal principles and facilitate encounters with the divine. The orientation, layout, and decoration of these structures were replete with symbolic significance, encoding esoteric knowledge and serving as conduits for spiritual power. For esoteric religious studies, the analysis of these symbols and their integration into ritual practice offers insights into the Egyptians' understanding of the divine, the afterlife, and the soul's adventure. The relationship between order and chaos, embodied in the struggle between the gods Ma'at and Isfet, vibes with esoteric themes of duality, transformation, and redemption. Similarly, the Egyptian concept of the afterlife, with its emphasis on judgment, moral accountability, and the possibility of eternal life, invites reflection on themes of justice, purity, and the soul's evolution. These themes, deeply embedded in Egyptian rituals and mythology, continue to inform contemporary spiritual practices and esoteric thought, underscoring the eternal relevance of ancient wisdom.

Furthermore, the integration of Greek practices into late Egyptian rituals during the Ptolemaic period exemplifies the dynamic nature of religious traditions, as they adapt to changing cultural and historical contexts. This syncretism, resulting in the blending of Egyptian and Greek gods, beliefs, and ritual practices, highlights the fluid bounds between religious traditions and the potential for cross-cultural exchange and innovation in the spiritual domain.

The study of ancient Egyptian rituals and symbolism within esoteric religious studies opens a window onto a world where the sacred infused every aspect of life, all the way from the grandiose temples and pyramids reaching towards the heavens to the intricate amulets worn for protection and blessing. It reveals a civilization that, through its religious practices and symbolic language, sought to understand the mysteries of existence and secure its place within a universal order perceived as fundamentally good, just, and beautiful. As such, ancient Egyptian religion, with its opulent heritage of rituals, myths, and symbols, remains a living source of encouragement and insight for those seeking to explore the depths of the esoteric tradition.

Here we explore a myriad topics within the larger framework of ancient Egyptian rituals and symbolism. It's going to be a long ride, like being in a boat traveling down the Nile. Let's begin, shall we?

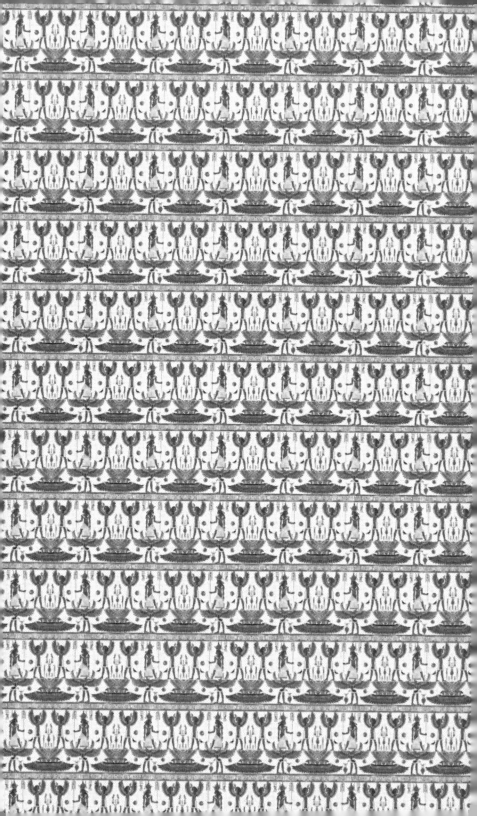

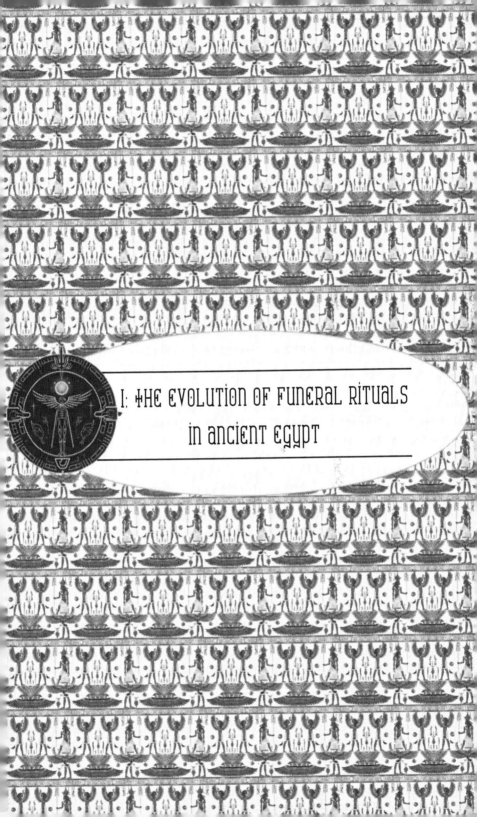

I: THE EVOLUTION OF FUNERAL RITUALS in ANCIENT EGYPT

The funeral rituals of Ancient Egypt, a civilization renowned for its monumental architecture, hieroglyphic script, and complex pantheon, stand for one of the most intricate and symbolically opulent aspects of their culture. These ceremonies, evolving over millennia, were not merely about mourning the dead but were deeply imbued with religious significance, reflecting the Egyptians' beliefs in the afterlife, resurrection, and eternal life. The evolution of these rituals, all the way from the Predynastic period through the Old, Middle, and New Kingdoms, and into the Late Period, shows the Egyptians' changing views on death, the soul's adventure, and the afterlife, as well as shifts in social structures, political power, and religious practices.

In the Predynastic period, before the unification of Egypt around 3100 BCE, burials were relatively simple. The dead were interred in shallow pits in the desert, often in a fetal position, which was believed to resemble the posture of birth, symbolizing death as a rebirth into the afterlife. Grave goods, though modest, were included: pottery, personal adornments, and food offerings, suggesting a belief in an afterlife where these items would be needed. This period laid the foundational belief in the afterlife that would become a central tenet of Egyptian religion and culture. With the unification of Egypt and the rise of the pharaohs in the Early Dynastic Period, funeral rituals became more elaborate, reflecting the increasing social stratification and the pharaoh's divine status. The construction of mastabas, flat-roofed, rectangular tombs with underground burial chambers, marked a significant evolution in burial practices. These were for the elite, indicating a belief that the afterlife's quality was linked to one's social status and the grandeur of one's tomb. The concept of ka, one of the components of the soul of humanity, which needed sustenance even after death, became integral to Egyptian funerary practices, leading to the inclusion of more elaborate offerings and the construction of offering tables within tombs.

The Old Kingdom, often called the Age of the Pyramids, saw the zenith of Egyptian tomb architecture and the complexity of funerary rituals. The pyramids, monumental tombs for the pharaohs, were seen as stairs to the heavens, allowing the king to join the gods in the afterlife. The Pyramid Texts, the oldest known religious texts in the world, inscribed within the pyramids of Unas and following rulers, contained spells, prayers, and incantations intended to protect the pharaoh's soul (ba) and guide it through the Duat, or underworld, to the afterlife. These texts uncover the Egyptians' increasingly complex views of the afterlife and the dangers the soul faced on its adventure, requiring magical protection and guidance.

During the Middle Kingdom, funerary practices democratized somewhat, reflecting changes in religious beliefs and social structures. The Coffin Texts, successors to the Pyramid Texts, were inscribed on the coffins of officials and later, on those of non-royals, suggesting a belief that not just the pharaoh but also commoners could aspire to a favorable afterlife. These texts emphasized moral integrity and the heart's place, judged against the feather of Ma'at (truth and order) in the Hall of Two Truths. This period saw the development of the Book of the Dead, a collection of spells and instructions to ensure safe passage through the underworld, which would become a key element of Egyptian funerary practices.

The New Kingdom saw the apogee of Egyptian power and the further elaboration of funerary rituals. Tombs in the Valley of the Kings, with their elaborate wall paintings and carvings, reflect the period's artistry and religious fervor. The Book of the Dead, now written on papyrus and placed in the tomb, detailed the deceased's adventure through the underworld, emphasizing the importance of the funerary rites performed by the living to ensure the deceased's resurrection and immortality. The rituals performed by priests, including the Opening of the Mouth ceremony, were believed to reanimate the mummy, allowing it to breathe, eat, and speak in the afterlife. These practices underscore the Egyptians' belief in the power of ritual and magic to go beyond death.

In the Late Period, as Egypt faced periods of foreign domination and internal strife, there was a resurgence in the emphasis on personal piety and the individual's relationship with the gods in funerary practices. Burials often included amulets and magical objects intended to protect the deceased in the afterlife, reflecting an amalgamation of traditional beliefs and newer religious influences. The democratization of the afterlife continued, with texts and amulets previously reserved for royalty becoming more widely available. Throughout these periods, the place of the funerary deity Osiris became increasingly central. Originally a god of fertility, Osiris' myth, involving his death, dismemberment, and resurrection by Isis, his wife, became a powerful symbol of the afterlife's promise of rebirth and eternal life. By identifying with Osiris, the deceased hoped to overcome death and live forever in the Field of Reeds, a paradisiacal version of Egypt.

The evolution of funeral rituals in Ancient Egypt reflects a civilization deeply engaged with questions of mortality, the afterlife, and the divine. From the simplest desert burials to the grand tombs of the Valley of the Kings, these practices were not static but evolved in response to changes in religious beliefs, social structures, and political power. They uncover the Egyptians' profound belief in the afterlife's existence, the importance of the rituals performed by the living for the dead, and the hope for resurrection and eternal life. These beliefs and practices, inscribed on tomb walls, written on papyrus, and embodied in the mummified remains of the dead, continue to fascinate and inform our understanding of this ancient civilization.

In examining the evolution of funeral rituals in Ancient Egypt, one appreciates the depth and complexity of their religious beliefs and their profound effect on Egyptian culture. These practices, opulent in symbolism and meaning, offer insight into the Egyptians' worldview, their understanding of death and the afterlife, and their unyielding quest for immortality. The study of these rituals, therefore, is not merely an academic pursuit but a window into the soul of Ancient Egypt, revealing a civilization that, through its rituals and beliefs, sought to conquer death and ensure eternal life for its people. The study of Ancient Egyptian funeral rituals and their evolution provides a comprehensive understanding of how the ancient Egyptians viewed the afterlife and the importance they placed on rituals to secure a place in the eternal world. By analyzing the changing practices over time, one can trace the shifts in religious thought, societal structure, and the personal aspirations of the Egyptians towards achieving immortality. This opulent atlas of belief and ritual underscores the Egyptians' profound relationship with the divine, their dead, and their lasting quest for eternal life, making it a fascinating subject for scholars and laypersons alike interested in the intersections of religion, history, and anthropology.

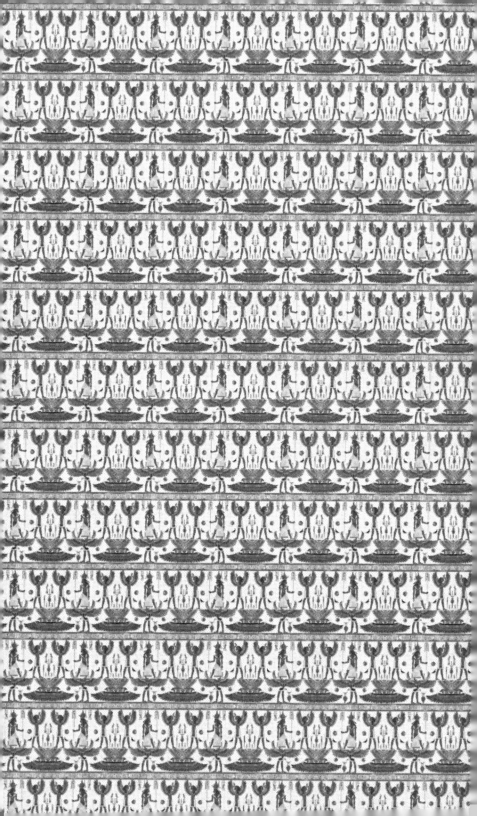

II: SYMBOLISM IN EGYPTIAN TEMPLE ARCHITECTURE

The architecture of Ancient Egyptian temples is a confirmation of a civilization deeply entrenched in the symbolic representation of its religious beliefs, cosmology, and the divine order of the universe. These structures, far from being mere places of worship, were designed as tangible manifestations of the world's creation, the gods' abode, and the afterlife, embodying the intersection between the earthly and the divine. The symbolism embedded within temple architecture, all the way from the grand pylons to the sacred inner sanctums, reflects the Ancient Egyptians' intricate belief system, their understanding of universal order, and their rituals and practices aimed at sustaining the universe's balance.

The design and orientation of Egyptian temples were profoundly symbolic, adhering to a universal blueprint that mirrored the Egyptians' universe. Temples were often aligned along an east-west axis, reflecting the sun's daily adventure, with the temple entrance facing east to greet the rising sun. This orientation was not merely practical but deeply symbolic, as the sun was associated with the god Ra, the creator deity, symbolizing rebirth, renewal, and the cyclical nature of life and the afterlife. The temple's layout, from its entrance to its innermost sanctuary, was a deliberate adventure from the world of the living to the divine world, echoing the sun's passage across the sky and through the underworld. The temple's pylon, the monumental gateway, symbolized the horizon where the sun rises and sets, marking the boundary between the human and divine worlds. This towering entrance, often adorned with reliefs of the pharaoh smiting his enemies, underscored the ruler's place as the earthly embodiment of divine order, protector of Egypt, and mediator between the gods and humanity. Beyond the pylon lay the temple's open courtyard, bathed in sunlight, representing the primordial waters from which the world was created. This space, accessible to the laity during festivals, symbolized the emergence of order from chaos, a central theme in Egyptian cosmology. The hypostyle hall, with its forest of towering columns, often followed the open courtyard. The columns, resembling papyrus and lotus plants, the symbols of Upper and Lower Egypt, respectively, signified the fecundity of the Nile and the country's unity. The ceiling, decorated with astronomical symbols, stars, and vultures spreading their wings, represented the sky, with the columns as the marshes from which the primeval mound emerged at the beginning of time. This hall, dimly lit, marked the transition from the outer world to the more sacred spaces of the temple, a threshold between the earthly and the divine.

Deeper within the temple lay the sanctuary, the most sacred space, housing the cult statue of the deity to whom the temple was dedicated. This innermost chamber, often lit by a single opening, symbolized the primeval darkness from which creation emerged. The statue itself, made from precious materials and ritually animated through the Opening of the Mouth ceremony, was not merely an idol but an embodiment of the god's living essence on earth. The sanctuary, as the temple's holiest part, represented the point of creation, the eternal home of the deity, and the focal point of the temple's religious ceremonies.

Adjacent to the sanctuary were various side chambers used for storing ritual implements, offerings, and the wealth amassed by the temple. These rooms, though utilitarian, were integral to the temple's function as a living religious institution and the economic center of its surrounding region. The temple walls, covered in reliefs and hieroglyphs, depicted the pharaoh's interactions with the gods, ritual ceremonies, and mythological scenes, serving both a religious function and reinforcing the pharaoh's divine right to rule. The symbolism in Egyptian temple architecture extended to the temple's exterior as well. Obelisks, tall, four-sided, tapered monuments topped with a pyramidion, stood at temple entrances or were erected in pairs before the pylon. These stone spires, gleaming in the sun, symbolized the sun's rays, reinforcing the temple's connection to Ra and the solar aspects of other gods. Similarly, the temple's outer walls,

often encircled by a massive mud-brick enclo-
sure, demarcated the sacred space from the pro-
fane, creating a symbolic boundary between order (ma'at) and chaos (isfet).

The temple complex also included sacred
lakes, symbolic of the primordial waters of creation, where priests performed purification rituals before entering the temple to perform their
duties. These waters, reflective of the sky, linked
the temple not just to the creation myth but also
to the annual flooding of the Nile, which was
essential for the renewal of Egypt's land and the
prosperity of its people. The symbolism in
Egyptian temple architecture reveals a profound
connection between the physical structures and
the Egyptians' religious beliefs, cosmological
views, and ritual practices. These temples were
designed as microcosms of the universe, embodying the creation myth, the gods' abode, and
the eternal cycle of life, death, and rebirth.
Through their architecture, the Ancient Egyptians expressed their understanding of the divine order, the pharaoh's place as the intermediary between gods and humans, and the eternal
struggle between order and chaos.

In exploring the symbolism of Egyptian
temple architecture, one gains insight into the
Ancient Egyptians' worldview, their religious
practices, and the place of the temple as a nexus
between the divine and the earthly. The temples,
through their design, orientation, and decora-

tion, were not merely buildings but sacred spaces that held a central place in sustaining the cosmos, serving as gateways to the divine, and ensuring the continuity of ma'at, the fundamental order of the universe. This intricate relationship between architecture and symbolism underscores the Egyptians' belief in the power of the physical world to reflect and affect the divine world, a confirmation of their profound spirituality and religious fervor.

The study of Ancient Egyptian temple architecture, therefore, is not just an examination of physical structures but an adventure into the heart of Egyptian religious thought, cosmology, and the place of the divine in everyday life. These temples, as lasting symbols of the Ancient Egyptians' quest for understanding and harmony with the universe, continue to allure scholars and laypersons alike, offering eternal insights into one of history's most fascinating civilizations. Through their monumental architecture and the symbolism that permeates every stone, the Ancient Egyptian temples remain a profound expression of humanity's eternal quest to comprehend the divine and its place within the cosmos.

The symbolism in Egyptian temple architecture provides a comprehensive lens through which to view the ancient Egyptians' religious and cosmological beliefs. It shows a civilization that saw their gods in everything around them, all the way from the rising sun to the fertile Nile, and sought to embody these divine aspects in their sacred spaces. The temples of Ancient Egypt, through their symbolic architecture, served not just as places of worship but as embodiments of the universal order, reflecting the Egyptians' deep spiritual connection with their gods, the universe, and the eternal cycle of life and rebirth.

III: †HE PHARAOH IN RELIGIOUS CEREMONIES

The place of the pharaoh in Ancient Egyptian religious ceremonies was paramount, embodying the intersection of the divine and the terrestrial, a bridge between the gods and the people. As both a god and a ruler, the pharaoh's responsibilities extended beyond the administrative and military worlds into the spiritual and religious life of Ancient Egypt. This dual place was fundamental to Egyptian theology and cosmology, with the pharaoh acting as the key figure in maintaining ma'at, the universal order and balance, through his participation in religious ceremonies and rituals. These practices were not merely symbolic but were respected as essential acts that sustained the universe, ensured the Nile's fertility, and guaranteed the prosperity and wellness of the kingdom.

The pharaoh's divine status was grounded in Egyptian mythology. He was often regarded as the son of Ra, the sun god, or as the incarnation of Horus, the falcon-headed god who represented kingship and protection. This divine lineage established the pharaoh as the chosen intermediary between the gods and the Egyptian people. His place in religious ceremonies, therefore, was not just as a participant but as a conduit through which the divine will could be manifested on Earth. The rituals performed by the pharaoh were seen as renewing the gods' blessings upon the land, reaffirming his divine right to rule, and perpetuating the universal order.

One of the most significant religious ceremonies involving the pharaoh was the Sed festival, also known as the Heb Sed, a jubilee festival traditionally celebrated after thirty years of a pharaoh's reign and subsequently every three to four years. This festival was intended to rejuvenate the pharaoh's strength and vitality, thereby renewing his ability to rule effectively. During the Sed festival, the pharaoh performed a series of rituals and physical challenges, including a symbolic race around a boundary stone course, to demonstrate his fitness to continue as king and his capacity to maintain ma'at. This ceremony not just reinforced the pharaoh's divine nature but also served as a public reaffirmation of his bond with the gods and his undiminished powers. The daily temple rituals were another aspect of the pharaoh's religious duties, although in practice, these were often carried out by priests acting on his behalf. The most important of these was the offering ceremony, where the pharaoh, or the priest acting in his stead, presented offerings of food, drink, and incense to the gods' statues. This ritual was essential for appeasing the gods, ensuring their continued favor, and enabling them to partake of the essence of the offerings, thus sustaining them. The pharaoh's place in these ceremonies was as the supreme priest of every temple in Egypt, underscoring his unparalleled position in Egyptian religion and society. In addition to these rituals, the pharaoh also held a necessary place in the construction and consecration of temples, acts imbued with religious significance. Temples were seen as the earthly dwellings of the gods, and their construction was a sacred act, often initiated by the pharaoh to honor a deity and ensure their favor. The pharaoh was involved in the foundation ceremonies, which included the ritual of stretching the cord, aligning the temple with the stars to ensure divine protection and blessings. Through these acts, the pharaoh was seen as a builder of the universal order, further solidifying his divine status and his place as the protector of Egypt's religious and social harmony.

The pharaoh's involvement in funerary rituals, particularly those of the royal family and other high-ranking officials, was another aspect of his religious duties. These rituals, designed to secure a safe passage to the afterlife for the deceased, often featured the pharaoh making offerings to Osiris, the god of the dead and resurrection. The pharaoh's participation underscored the belief in the afterlife's importance and his place in ensuring the deceased's transition from the earthly world to the divine. The pharaoh's presence was also central to the various festivals celebrated throughout the year, which were necessary for sustaining the social and universal order. These festivals, including the Beautiful Festival of the Valley, the Opet Festival, and the Festival of Min, involved processions, offerings, and celebrations that reinforced the bonds between the gods, the pharaoh, and the people. Through his participation, the pharaoh not just demonstrated his devotion to the gods but also facilitated the communal sharing of the divine blessing with the populace, ensuring the kingdom's prosperity and stability.

The place of the pharaoh in religious ceremonies was, therefore, multifaceted, encompassing aspects of ritual performance, temple construction, and participation in festivals that were integral to the maintenance of ma'at and the prosperity of Egypt. His participation in these ceremonies was not merely a duty but a sacred obligation, reflecting his unique position as both a divine and earthly ruler. Through these rituals, the pharaoh reaffirmed his divine status, ensured the gods' favor, and maintained the universal order upon which the wellness of Egypt depended.

This relationship between the pharaoh and the divine, mediated through religious ceremonies, underscored the inherently theological nature of Egyptian kingship. The pharaoh was not just a ruler but a god among men, whose actions directly influenced the universal balance and the welfare of his people. The rituals he performed or sponsored were living links between the divine and the mundane, ensuring the continuous flow of divine blessings to the land and its people. In this way, the religious ceremonies and the pharaoh's place within them were central to the ideological and theological underpinnings of Ancient Egyptian civilization.

The study of the pharaoh's place in religious ceremonies offers invaluable insights into Ancient Egyptian religion, politics, and society, revealing the complex relationship between divine authority and earthly power. It highlights the pharaoh's necessary place in sustaining the universe's order, the profound spiritual responsibilities vested in his office, and the symbolic acts through which he communicated with the gods and mediated their will on Earth. Through these ceremonies, the pharaoh not just maintained his divine status and the legitimacy of his rule but also ensured the prosperity and stability of Egypt, reflecting the deep interconnection between religion and governance in Ancient Egyptian civilization. In examining the pharaoh's place in religious ceremonies, one gains a deeper understanding of the theological principles that governed Ancient Egyptian thought, the symbolic language through which they articulated their relationship with the divine, and the ceremonial practices that shaped their world. The pharaoh, as the central figure in this religious territory, embodied the fusion of humanity's and divine, acting as the keystone in the arch of Egyptian religious and societal structure. His actions, whether in the construction of temples, the performance of rituals, or the celebration of festivals, were manifestations of the divine will, ensuring the continuity of the cosmos and the eternal prosperity of his world.

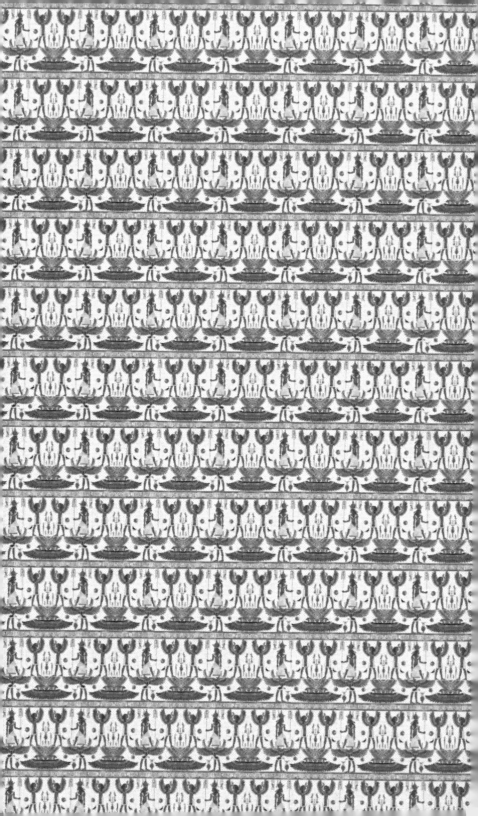

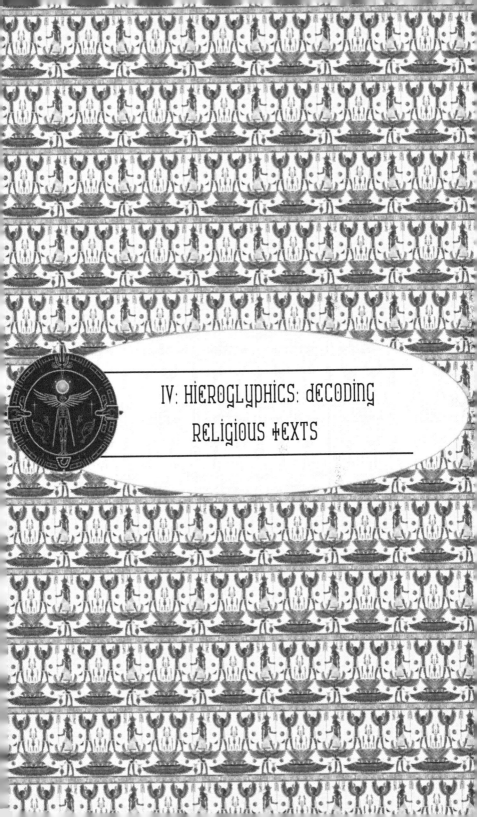

IV: HIEROGLYPHICS: DECODING RELIGIOUS TEXTS

Hieroglyphics, the writing system of ancient Egypt, stands as a profound confirmation of a civilization deeply engaged with the divine, the mystical, and the eternal. This script, composed of pictorial symbols, was not merely a means of communication but a sacred language that encoded the religious beliefs, rituals, and cosmology of the Ancient Egyptians. The task of decoding these religious texts, inscribed on temple walls, papyrus scrolls, and tomb chambers, offers a window into the spiritual life of this ancient civilization, revealing the complexities of their theology, the rituals they performed, and the gods they worshipped.

The hieroglyphic script, developed around 3200 BCE, was used primarily for religious and ceremonial purposes throughout most of its history. It consisted of over seven hundred signs, including phonetic symbols, ideograms, and determinatives, which provided clues to the meaning of the words they accompanied. This script was believed to have been invented by the god Thoth, the deity of wisdom, writing, and magic, underscoring its divine origin and sacred nature. Hieroglyphs were respected as the words of the gods (medu neter), imbued with power and magic, and their use was central to the Egyptians' religious practices and beliefs. The decoding of religious texts written in hieroglyphics has revealed much about Egyptian theology, including the creation myths that formed the basis of their cosmology. These texts describe the world's creation from the primordial chaos, the emergence of the gods, and the establishment of ma'at, the universal order. The Pyramid Texts, among the oldest religious texts in the world, inscribed in the pyramids of the Old Kingdom pharaohs, contain spells, hymns, and prayers intended to protect the deceased king's soul and guide it to the afterlife. These texts provide insights into the Egyptians' beliefs about death, the afterlife, and the soul's adventure through the Duat, the underworld.

The Coffin Texts, which followed the Pyramid Texts and were inscribed on the coffins of officials and later, commoners, expanded the possibility of an afterlife beyond the royal family to include a broader segment of Egyptian society. These texts, with their spells for the dead to use in the afterlife, illustrate the democratization of religion in ancient Egypt, allowing individuals outside the royal family to access the spells and guidance necessary for a successful adventure through the Duat.

The Book of the Dead, perhaps the most famous of the ancient Egyptian religious texts, was a collection of spells, prayers, and incantations designed to guide the deceased through the underworld and into the afterlife. Written on papyrus and placed in the tomb, the Book of the Dead illustrates the Egyptians' complex beliefs about death and the afterlife, including the judgment of the soul, the importance of the heart, and the trials the deceased would face before reaching the Field of Reeds, a paradisiacal version of Egypt.

The decoding of hieroglyphics also sheds light on the Egyptians' pantheon and the complex relationships between the gods. Temple inscriptions, like those found in Karnak, Luxor, and other monumental religious sites, detail the gods' myths, their interactions with each other, and the rituals performed in their honor. These texts uncover the Egyptians' polytheistic beliefs, the attributes and powers of the gods, and the importance of rituals and offerings in sustaining the gods and ensuring their favor. The religious texts inscribed in hieroglyphics were not solely focused on the afterlife and the gods but also contained instructions for rituals, hymns of praise, and magical spells. These texts provide a comprehensive view of the Egyptians' religious practices, all the way from the daily rituals performed by priests in the temples to the annual festivals celebrated by the populace. They underscore the centrality of religion in ancient Egyptian society and the place of the pharaoh as both a religious and political leader, responsible for maintaining ma'at and ensuring the gods' favor.

The process of decoding these religious texts has been a monumental task, beginning with the Rosetta Stone's discovery in 1799, which provided the key to understanding hieroglyphics. The work of scholars and Egyptologists in translating these texts has opened up a giant field of study, revealing the depth and richness of ancient Egyptian religious thought, their conception of the divine, and their rituals and practices. The study of hieroglyphics and the decoding of ancient Egyptian religious texts is not merely an academic exercise but an adventure into the heart of a civilization that saw the divine in every aspect of the world around them. These texts offer insights into the Egyptians' worldview, their understanding of life, death, and the afterlife, and the profound sense of continuity and eternal life that pervaded their culture. Through these ancient words, inscribed in stone and papyrus, the ancient Egyptians speak to us of their gods, their rituals, and their unshakable belief in a life beyond death, providing an eternal confirmation of their search for meaning and their quest for immortality.

In short, the place of hieroglyphics in encoding the religious texts of ancient Egypt cannot be overstated. These sacred symbols, believed to be the words of the gods themselves, offer a direct link to the spiritual life of this ancient civilization, revealing the complexities of their theology, the rituals they practiced, and their beliefs about the afterlife. The task of decoding these texts has allowed modern scholars to reconstruct the religious territory of ancient

Egypt, offering insights into the ways in which the Egyptians understood the world and their place within it. Through these ancient inscriptions, we gain a deeper understanding of a civilization that, through its religious beliefs and practices, sought to go beyond the mortal world and achieve a form of eternal life. The study of hieroglyphics and the religious texts they encode is thus a window into the soul of ancient Egypt, illuminating the spiritual quest that lay at the heart of one of history's most lasting civilizations.

V: THE NILE RIVER IN EGYPTIAN RITUALS

The Nile River, flowing through the heart of ancient Egypt, was more than a source of water; it was the lifeblood of a civilization and a symbol of universal order and renewal. Its significance permeated every aspect of Egyptian life, especially its religious rituals and practices. The annual flooding of the Nile, known as the inundation, was seen as a divine manifestation, a renewal of the land's fertility, and by extension, the rebirth of the cosmos itself. This natural cycle was deeply intertwined with the Egyptians' religious beliefs, cosmology, and rituals, making the Nile not just a river in the physical territory but a central element in the spiritual and symbolic territory of ancient Egypt.

The inundation was closely associated with the myth of Osiris, the god of the afterlife, rebirth, and the Nile's fertility. According to myth, Osiris was killed and dismembered by his brother Set, and his body parts were scattered across Egypt. His wife, Isis, retrieved and reassembled his body, and Osiris was resurrected, becoming the ruler of the afterlife. The scattering and reassembling of Osiris' body were symbolically linked to the dispersal and gathering of the Nile's waters, and the annual inundation was seen as Osiris' tears of joy at being reunited with Isis, bringing fertility to the land. This mythological scaffolding underscored the Nile's place in the cycles of death and rebirth, both in the agricultural cycle and the human adventure through the afterlife.

Rituals associated with the inundation were central to Egyptian religious practice. The most important of these was the Wepet Renpet festival, or the Opening of the Year, which celebrated the New Year and the Nile's flood. This festival was not just a time of joy and celebration but also a period of intense religious activity, during which the Egyptians performed rituals to honor the gods and ensure that the inundation would bring sufficient water to irrigate the fields. The flood's onset was monitored from the Nilometer, a structure used to measure the Nile's water level, and the measurements were used to predict the coming agricultural season's success, further linking the river to the Egyptians' economic and spiritual wellness. Temples along the Nile held a necessary place in these rituals, serving as centers for the worship of the gods associated with the river and fertility. The most significant of these deities was Hapi, the god of the Nile, often depicted as a man with a pot-belly, symbolizing abundance, bearing aquatic plants. Offerings and sacrifices were made to Hapi to appease him and to ensure a bountiful flood. These offerings included flowers, incense, and food, which were either placed in the river or at altars within the temples. The rituals performed in honor of Hapi and the Nile were not merely acts of devotion but were believed to have a direct effect on the river's behavior, influencing the gods to bring about a flood that was neither too low, leading to famine, nor too high, causing destruction.

The Nile also held a significant place in funerary rituals and beliefs about the afterlife. The river was seen as a metaphor for the adventure to the afterlife, with the west bank, where the sun set and where most tombs were located, representing the world of the dead. Funerary processions often involved crossing the Nile from east to west, symbolizing the deceased's transition from the world of the living to the afterlife. The river thus served as a physical and symbolic boundary between life and death, reinforcing the Egyptians' belief in the afterlife and the cyclical nature of existence. Also, the Nile's water was used in purification rituals, both in daily life and in religious ceremonies. Priests would cleanse themselves with Nile water before performing rituals or entering temples, a practice that underscored the river's sacredness and its association with purity and renewal. Water from the Nile was also used in the mummification process, further linking the river to death, rebirth, and the afterlife.

The significance of the Nile in Egyptian rituals and symbolism reflects the river's integral place in the civilization's survival and prosperity. It was a source of life, a symbol of fertility and rebirth, and a pathway to the afterlife, deeply charted into the map of Egyptian religious beliefs and practices. The rituals associated with the Nile, all the way from the celebrations of the inundation to the funerary rites, were expressions of the Egyptians' understanding of the cosmos, their dependence on the natural world, and their quest for harmony with the divine.

In essence, the Nile River was not merely a physical feature of the territory but a divine entity, central to the Egyptians' worldview and religious practices. Its cyclical flood pattern was a powerful symbol of regeneration, renewal, and the eternal cycle of life and death, themes that resonated deeply with the Egyptian people and their rulers. Through their rituals and myths, the ancient Egyptians expressed their reverence for the Nile, recognizing its necessary place in sustaining their civilization and connecting them with the divine. The river's presence in Egyptian religious rituals and symbolism underscores the profound bond between the natural world and the spiritual, a relationship that defined much of ancient Egyptian culture and continues to fascinate modern scholars and enthusiasts alike. The study of the Nile's significance in Egyptian rituals and symbolism offers invaluable insights into the ancient Egyptians' religious beliefs, their cosmology, and their daily lives. It reveals a civilization that saw the divine in the natural world, celebrated the cycles of nature, and sought to live in harmony with the cosmos. The Nile, with

its life-giving waters and its central place in
Egyptian mythology and ritual practice, stands
as a confirmation of the ancient Egyptians' reverence for the natural world and their profound
understanding of the interconnections between
the physical and the spiritual. Through the rituals and beliefs associated with the Nile, we gain a
deeper appreciation for ancient Egyptian civilization, its spirituality, and its lasting heritage.

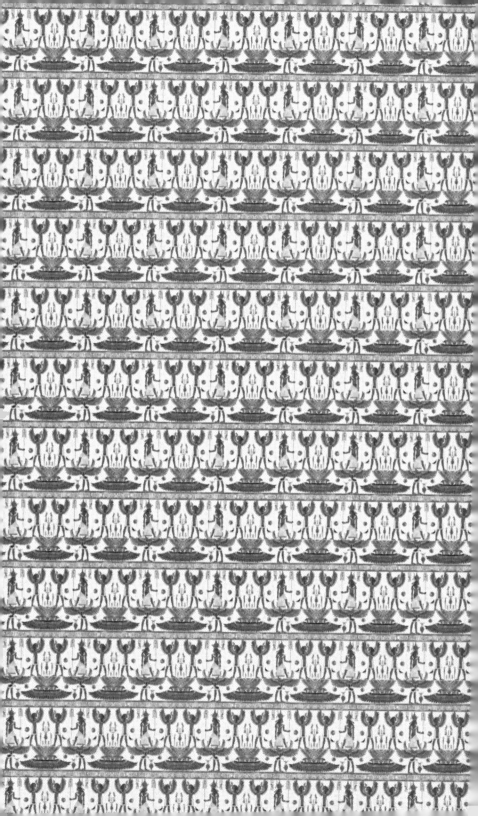

VI: GODS AND GODDESSES

The pantheon of ancient Egyptian deities is a vivid reflection of the civilization's opulent and multifaceted culture, embodying the complexities of their cosmology, natural phenomena, societal norms, and the profound mysteries of life and death. This comprehensive study gets into the roles, relationships, and symbolism of these gods and goddesses, illustrating how they were not mere figments of religious imagination but integral to the Egyptians' understanding of the world around them and their place within it.

Central to the Egyptian pantheon was Ra, the sun god, a deity of paramount importance who symbolized creation, resurrection, and the cycle of day and night. Ra's daily adventure across the sky in his solar boat was a manifestation of the universal order, with his rebirth at dawn representing the triumph of light over darkness, order over chaos. The myth of Ra's nightly passage through the underworld, where he defeated the serpent Apophis, underscored the eternal struggle between order and chaos, a theme central to Egyptian religious thought.

Osiris, the god of the afterlife, resurrection, and fertility, was another necessary figure in the Egyptian pantheon. His myth, involving death at the hands of his brother Set, dismemberment, and following resurrection by his wife Isis, encapsulated themes of death, regeneration, and the cyclical nature of life. Osiris became the embodiment of the afterlife, promising resurrection and eternal life to those who followed his teachings and upheld ma'at, the principle of universal order and balance. Isis, the wife of Osiris, was respected as the goddess of magic, motherhood, and healing. Her devotion to Osiris, demonstrated by her quest to reassemble his scattered body parts, made her a symbol of loyal love, the protective mother, and the healer. Her magical prowess, used to resurrect Osiris and protect their son Horus, endowed her with a reputation as a powerful sorceress whose aid could be invoked in times of need.

Horus, the son of Osiris and Isis, was depicted as a falcon-headed god, symbolizing kingship, the sky, and protection. The Pharaoh was respected as Horus incarnate, embodying the living god on earth. The struggle between Horus and Set for the throne of Egypt, resulting in Horus' victory, was a mythological reflection of the constant battle between order and disorder, legitimizing the pharaoh's rule as the upholder of ma'at. Set, the god of chaos, storms, and the desert, was often cast as the antagonist in Egyptian mythology, particularly in the story of Osiris' murder and Horus' following battle for justice. Despite his negative aspects, Set was also recognized for his place in protecting Ra during his nightly adventure through the underworld, demonstrating the dual nature of many Egyptian deities who could embody both constructive and destructive forces.

Anubis, the jackal-headed god associated with mummification and the afterlife, was a guardian of the dead. His place in the weighing of the heart ceremony, where the hearts of the deceased were weighed against the feather of Ma'at to determine their worthiness for the afterlife, underscored the importance of ethical living and moral integrity in Egyptian society.

Thoth, the ibis-headed god of writing, knowledge, and wisdom, was believed to be the inventor of hieroglyphics and a mediator between the gods. His association with the moon and his place as the recorder of time and the universe's order made him a symbol of intellect and the keeper of divine knowledge. Hathor, the goddess of love, beauty, music, and joy, was often depicted as a cow or a woman with cow's ears, symbolizing fertility and motherhood. Hathor's cult was all over, reflecting the Egyptians' appreciation for the pleasures of life and the importance of fertility and procreation.

Sekhmet, the lioness goddess, represented the destructive force of the sun's heat and was respected as a warrior goddess and protector of the pharaohs. Her ferocity was believed to be appeased through rituals and offerings, demonstrating the Egyptians' attempts to harmonize with the potentially destructive aspects of nature.

These deities, among others in the giant Egyptian pantheon, were not isolated entities but part of a complex nexus of myths, relationships, and universal principles that mirrored the Egyptians' understanding of the world. The gods and goddesses were invoked in daily life through rituals, prayers, and offerings, underscoring their integral place in the Egyptians' personal and communal existence. Temples dedicated to these deities served as centers of worship and religious activity, where priests performed rituals to sustain the gods and invoke their favor.

The significance of these gods and goddesses extended beyond religious rituals into the Egyptians' artistic expressions, governance, and societal norms, reflecting a worldview in which the divine permeated every aspect of existence. The pharaoh's place as the intermediary between the gods and the people, the moral and ethical teachings derived from the myths, and the cosmological significance of the deities' actions and interactions all held a part in shaping ancient Egyptian civilization. The gods and goddesses of ancient Egypt were embodiments of the forces of nature, societal ideals, and the mysteries of existence, charted into an opulent atlas of mythology and religious practice. Their worship was a reflection of the Egyptians' attempt to understand and influence the world around them, ensuring harmony, prosperity, and continuity of life. Through the study of these deities and their significance, we gain insight into the ancient Egyptians' worldview, their values, and their lasting heritage. This comprehensive adventure of Egyptian deities not just enriches our understanding of ancient Egyptian religion but also highlights the universal quest for meaning, order, and connection to the divine that defines the experience of humanity.

VII: animal symbolism

In ancient Egyptian mythology, animals were not merely part of the natural territory but were imbued with profound symbolic significance, serving as embodiments of gods, manifestations of divine principles, and intermediaries between the human and supernatural worlds. This deep-seated reverence and symbolic use of animals is evident in the depiction of deities with animal forms, the use of animal hieroglyphs, and the incorporation of animals in rituals and religious iconography. The symbolic use of animals in Egyptian mythology reflects a complex relationship between the natural world and the spiritual, highlighting the Egyptians' nuanced understanding of their environment and its connection to the divine.

The falcon, with its keen sight and majestic flight, was associated with Horus, the god of kingship and the sky. The falcon's attributes of power, vigilance, and dominion over the land were seen as reflective of the pharaoh's place as the earthly embodiment of Horus, ruling over Egypt with divine authority. The Eye of Horus, a symbol of protection, healing, and wholeness, further illustrates the falcon's significance, embodying the concept of divine oversight and intervention.

Cats were respected for their grace, agility, and prowess in hunting, embodying qualities of independence, protection, and fertility. Bastet, the goddess of home, fertility, and childbirth, was often depicted as a lioness or as a woman with the head of a domestic cat, highlighting the duality of feline nature—both nurturing and fiercely protective. The all over veneration of cats in Egyptian society, including the practice of mummifying cats and the severe penalties for harming them, underscores their symbolic importance and the belief in their sacred attributes.

The jackal, an animal associated with the deserts surrounding the Nile and known for its scavenging habits, was symbolic of Anubis, the god of mummification and the afterlife. Anubis' association with the jackal mirrored the Egyptians' observations of jackals' tendency to lurk around cemeteries, leading to the belief that Anubis watched over the dead. Anubis' place in embalming and the weighing of the heart ceremony in the Hall of Ma'at focuses on the jackal's connotations of protection, guidance, and transition from life to the afterlife.

Crocodiles, both feared and respected, were associated with Sobek, the god of the Nile's fertility and strength, as well as the dangers lurking in its waters. The crocodile's dual nature as both a creator and destroyer mirrored the Nile itself, which was essential for life but could also be a source of peril. Sobek's worship, particularly in regions close to the Nile, underscores the Egyptians' respect for the crocodile's power and their desire to appease these formidable creatures.

The cow was venerated as a symbol of fertility and maternal care, associated with Hathor, the goddess of love, beauty, and music. Hathor was often depicted as a cow, a woman with cow's ears, or wearing a headdress featuring cow horns with a solar disk, symbolizing her place as a celestial deity and protector of women and children. The cow's importance in Egyptian society, as a source of nourishment and a symbol of life-giving abundance, reflects its integral place in the mythology and religious practices.

The scarab beetle held a unique place in Egyptian symbolism, associated with the sun god Ra and the concept of rebirth and regeneration. The scarab, or dung beetle, which rolls dung into a ball as food and as brooding chambers, was seen as an emblem of the sun's daily adventure across the sky, and of life emerging from the depths of the underworld. Scarabs were used as amulets, seals, and in burial contexts, symbolizing protection, transformation, and the eternal cycle of life and death.

Snakes, embodying both danger and protection, were complex symbols in Egyptian mythology. The cobra, associated with Wadjet, the protective goddess of Lower Egypt, was depicted on the pharaoh's crown, representing sovereign authority and divine protection. The Uraeus, the rearing cobra symbol, signified the pharaoh's power to ward off enemies and evil spirits. Conversely, the serpent Apophis was the embodiment of chaos and destruction, constantly threatening the universal order and the sun god Ra's daily rebirth.

These examples stand for only a fraction of the opulent atlas of animal symbolism in ancient Egyptian mythology, reflecting a culture deeply connected to the natural world and attuned to the spiritual significance of its inhabitants. The symbolic use of animals in Egyptian religious thought and practice illustrates the Egyptians' belief in the enmeshment of all aspects of existence, where animals served as links between the earthly and the divine, embodying the gods' powers, and participating in the maintenance of the universal order. Through the reverence and symbolic representation of animals, ancient Egyptians expressed their understanding of the world, the divine, and the moral and ethical principles governing life. Animals in Egyptian mythology were not mere symbols but were respected as living participants in the universal drama, embodying the divine will and actively engaging in the processes of creation, protection, and renewal. This symbiotic relationship between the Egyptians and the animal deities in their pantheon highlights a worldview in which spirituality and the natural environment were inextricably linked, with animals serving as a bridge between the human and the divine, the natural and the supernatural.

The study of animal symbolism in Egyptian mythology offers profound insights into the ancient Egyptians' mindset, their religious beliefs, and their interactions with the world around them. It reveals a civilization that saw divinity in the natural world, recognizing and venerating the sacred qualities of animals that embodied the gods' power on earth. This reverence for animals underscores the holistic approach the Egyptians took to religion and life, where the natural and the supernatural worlds were seamlessly intertwined, and the presence of the divine was manifest in the everyday world. Through their mythology and religious practices, the ancient Egyptians left a heritage of harmony with the natural world, a deep respect for the forces of life and death, and a pantheon of deities that continue to fascinate and encourage.

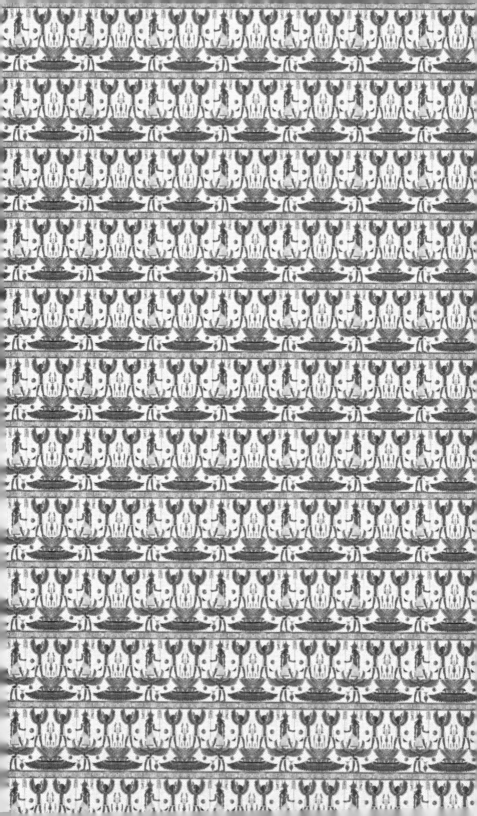

VIII: THE ART OF MUMMIFICATION: TECHNIQUES AND SYMBOLISM

The art of mummification in ancient Egypt is a profound confirmation of the civilization's beliefs in the afterlife, the soul's immortality, and the significance of the physical body in the spiritual adventure beyond death. This complex process, refined over millennia, was not merely a method of preserving the dead but was imbued with deep religious symbolism, reflecting the Egyptians' understanding of life, death, and rebirth. The techniques employed in mummification, along with the rituals and materials used, were opulent with symbolic meaning, aimed at ensuring the deceased's safe passage and acceptance into the afterlife.

Mummification in ancient Egypt evolved from simple pit burials in the Predynastic period, where the natural desiccation of the body in the hot, dry sand led to unintentional preservation. This natural mummification process likely influenced the development of artificial mummification techniques, as the Egyptians came to believe that preservation of the body was essential for the survival of the soul (ba) and the spirit (ka) in the afterlife. Over time, the Egyptians developed a sophisticated mummification process that involved the removal of internal organs, dehydration of the body, and wrapping in linen bandages, along with a series of religious rites. The first step in the mummification process was the removal of the internal organs, which were respected as sources of decay. The brain was removed through the nose using hooks, reflecting the belief that it was not essential for the afterlife, as the heart, thought to be the center of thought and emotion, was left in place. The liver, lungs, stomach, and intestines were removed, washed, and preserved separately in canopic jars, each protected by one of the Four Sons of Horus, deities who guarded the organs against decay and ensured their safety for the deceased's rebirth. The body was then desiccated using natron, a naturally occurring salt mixture, which dehydrated the body tissues and prevented decay. This process, lasting forty days, symbolized the purification and preparation of the body for its adventure to the afterlife. The use of natron was not merely practical but held deep symbolic significance, mirroring the transformative power of the desert's heat and dryness, which was believed to purify and sanctify the deceased. Following dehydration, the body was washed with water from the Nile, symbolizing rebirth and renewal, and then wrapped in hundreds of meters of linen bandages. The wrapping process was intricate and ritualized, with amulets and charms placed between the layers for protection and to ward off evil spirits. Among these, the scarab amulet, placed over the heart, was of particular importance, symbolizing rebirth and the sun's daily cycle. The Book of the Dead, a collection of spells and incantations, was often placed within the mummy wrappings or in the tomb, providing the deceased with the knowledge needed to navigate the afterlife. The final step in the mummification process was the ritual of the Opening of the Mouth, performed on both the mummy and the tomb statues. This ceremony, involving the use of special instruments to symbolically open the deceased's mouth, was believed to restore the senses and enable the deceased to breathe, eat, and speak in the afterlife. This ritual underscores the importance of the physical body in ancient Egyptian religious belief, as a vessel for the soul's adventure and a requisite for eternal life.

The art of mummification, with its complex blend of technical skill and religious ritual, reflects the ancient Egyptians' deep-seated beliefs in the afterlife and the necessity of preserving the body as a home for the soul. The materials and methods used were chosen for their symbolic meanings and their perceived ability to protect and sanctify the deceased. The extensive use of spells, amulets, and ritual ceremonies throughout the mummification process highlights the Egyptians' belief in the power of magic and the intervention of the gods in securing a favorable outcome in the afterlife.

Mummification was not simply a technique for preserving the dead but a deeply symbolic act that affirmed the deceased's identity, status, and beliefs. The process was a necessary element in the Egyptians' religious and cosmological worldview, embodying their understanding of death as a transition rather than an end, and the possibility of eternal life through rebirth. Through mummification, the Egyptians sought to go beyond the mortal world, ensuring that the deceased could continue to exist in the afterlife, participating in the universal order and enjoying the blessings of the gods.

The study of mummification provides invaluable insights into ancient Egyptian religion, society, and their profound respect for the dead. It reveals a civilization that viewed death as a doorway to a new existence, where the preservation of the body was essential for the continuity of life beyond the grave. The art of mummification, with its intricate techniques and opulent symbolism, stands as a confirmation of the ancient Egyptians' quest for immortality, reflecting their deep-seated beliefs in the afterlife and the lasting soul's adventure towards eternal life. Through this practice, the ancient Egyptians expressed their reverence for the divine, their understanding of the natural cycle of life and death, and their unstoppable hope for rebirth and renewal in the world beyond.

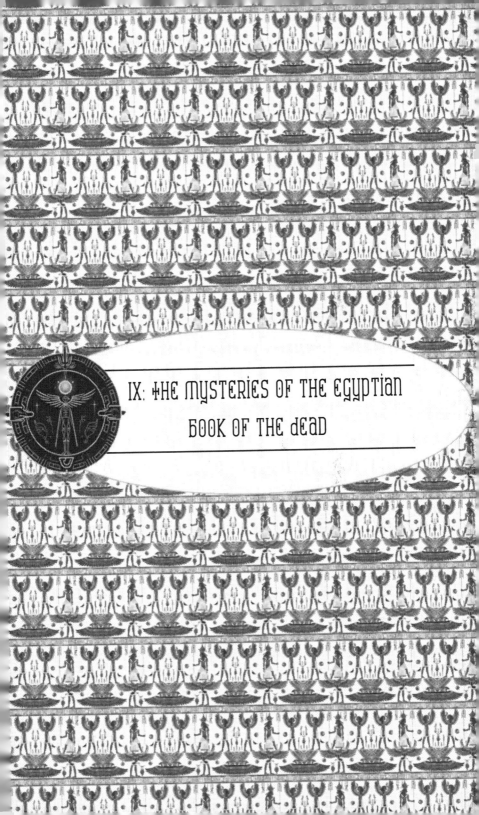

IX: THE MYSTERIES OF THE EGYPTIAN BOOK OF THE DEAD

The Egyptian Book of the Dead, known to the ancient Egyptians as the "Book of Coming Forth by Day," is a collection of spells, prayers, and incantations designed to guide the deceased through the underworld (Duat) and into the afterlife. Far from being a single uniform text, the Book of the Dead was a personalized document, often customized for the individual deceased, and varied significantly over time and between different versions. Its origins trace back to the Coffin Texts of the Middle Kingdom and the Pyramid Texts of the Old Kingdom, evolving into the form known today during the New Kingdom. The mysteries of the Book of the Dead lie not just in its content and purpose but also in its profound symbolism, its reflection of ancient Egyptian beliefs about death and the afterlife, and its influence on the broader cultural and religious territory of ancient Egypt.

The Book of the Dead served as a guide for the deceased, offering knowledge and protection through the various challenges of the underworld. The spells contained within it were believed to provide the knowledge necessary to navigate the dangers of the Duat, including demons and obstacles, and to appear before Osiris and the Forty-Two Judges in the Hall of Truth. Here, the deceased's heart was weighed against the feather of Ma'at, the goddess of truth and justice, in a symbolic judgment of their life's actions. The correct spells and declarations of innocence (the Negative Confessions) were necessary for passing this test, failing which the soul could be devoured by Ammit, the devourer of the dead, resulting in the second death, a fate respected as far worse than physical death.

The spells in the Book of the Dead also aimed to preserve the deceased's identity and memory, asserting the soul's continuity and its connection to the living world. They included declarations of the deceased's moral righteousness, achievements, and rightful place among the stars, reflecting the ancient Egyptians' belief in the importance of memory and heritage. The preservation of the body through mummification and the recitation of these spells were interconnected processes, both aimed at ensuring the deceased's immortality.

The symbolism within the Book of the Dead is opulent and varied, drawing from the natural world, everyday life, and religious beliefs to create a comprehensive cosmology of the afterlife. For example, the adventure of the sun god Ra through the underworld each night, battling the forces of chaos to rise again each morning, served as a metaphor for the deceased's hoped-for resurrection. The use of amulets, like the scarab for rebirth and the djed pillar for stability, placed within the mummy wrappings or inscribed with spells from the Book, provided magical protection and embodied the spells' power.

The Book of the Dead also reflects the ancient Egyptians' complex theology, which included a pantheon of gods and goddesses involved in the afterlife. The spells invoke deities like Thoth, the god of wisdom and writing, who was believed to record the outcome of the judgment; Anubis, the jackal-headed god who embalmed the dead and guarded the scales of justice; and Osiris, the lord of the underworld and the judge of the dead. The interaction between the deceased and these deities, mediated through the spells and rituals, underscores the Egyptians' belief in a deeply interconnected universe where human actions had universal significance. The creation and use of the Book of the Dead were deeply personalized, reflecting the individual's social status, wealth, and personal beliefs. While initially reserved for royalty and the elite, over time, the spells became more widely accessible, reflecting a democratization of afterlife beliefs. This shift illustrates the fluid nature of ancient Egyptian religious practices and the adaptation of religious texts to meet the needs of a changing society.

The mysteries of the Book of the Dead, therefore, lie not just in its content but in its capacity to uncover the depth of ancient Egyptian spirituality and their conception of the afterlife. It offers a window into how the ancient Egyptians understood their place in the universe, the nature of the soul, and the possibility of life beyond death. The Book of the Dead stands as a monument to the ancient Egyptians' quest for immortality, encapsulating their beliefs, hopes, and fears about the afterlife in a collection of texts that continue to fascinate and encourage.

In studying the Book of the Dead, scholars and enthusiasts alike are drawn into the opulent atlas of ancient Egyptian religious thought, where the bounds between the physical and spiritual worlds were fluid, and death was but a transition to a new state of being. The Book of the Dead thus remains a key to decoding the mysteries of ancient Egyptian religion, offering insights into their rituals, cosmology, and the profound belief in a life beyond death that shaped their civilization. Through its spells and incantations, the Book of the Dead communicates the ancient Egyptians' lasting desire to go beyond mortality, to live on in the collective memory of the living, and to achieve eternal life in the world of the gods.

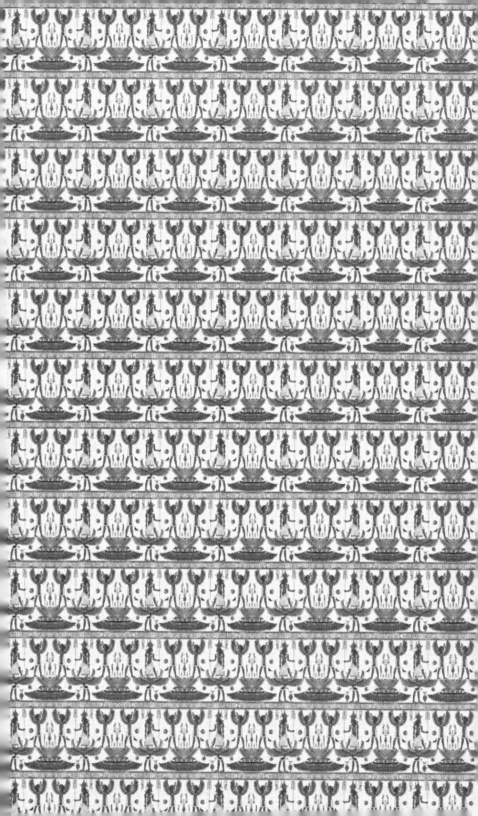

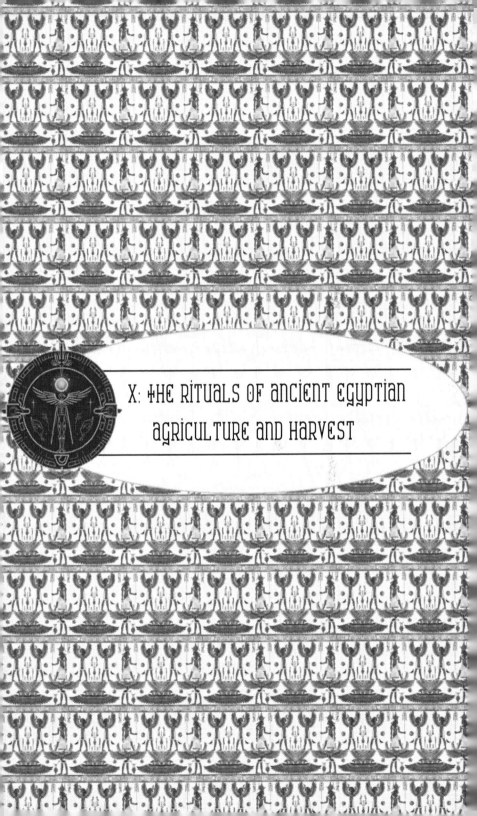

X: THE RITUALS OF ANCIENT EGYPTIAN AGRICULTURE AND HARVEST

The rituals of ancient Egyptian agriculture and harvest were deeply intertwined with the civilization's cosmology, religious beliefs, and the annual flooding of the Nile River, which was the lifeblood of Egypt's agricultural prosperity. These rituals were not mere ceremonial acts but were seen as living processes that ensured the fertility of the land, the success of the crops, and by extension, the survival and prosperity of the people. The Egyptians believed that the harmonious relationship between the heavens, the earth, and the underworld held a necessary place in the agricultural cycle, and thus, their rituals were designed to honor the gods, seek their blessings, and ensure the continuation of the natural order.

At the heart of ancient Egyptian agricultural rituals was the worship of Osiris, the god of the afterlife, vegetation, and fertility. The myth of Osiris, who was murdered by his brother Set and then resurrected by his wife Isis, was symbolic of the death and rebirth cycle of nature. Osiris was closely associated with the Nile's inundation, which brought the necessary silt and water to rejuvenate the land. The rituals performed in his honor, particularly during the inundation and planting seasons, were aimed at invoking his essence to ensure the land's fertility and the crops' growth.

One of the key rituals was the 'Flooding of the Nile' ceremony, which celebrated the river's annual flood. This event was necessary for washing nutrient-opulent silt onto the farmlands, and its onset was eagerly anticipated by the farmers. The inundation was seen as a manifestation of Osiris' powers, and its arrival was marked by festive ceremonies that included offerings, hymns, and prayers to Osiris and other deities associated with the Nile and fertility, like Hapi, the god of the Nile's flood. These ceremonies were not just expressions of gratitude but also pleas for the flood to reach the optimal level—neither too low, which would result in famine, nor too high, which could bring destruction. Following the retreat of the floodwaters, the land was plowed and seeds were sown, a process that was also accompanied by rituals. The 'Breaking of the Ground' ceremony involved the symbolic plowing of the first furrow by a figure of authority, often represented by the Pharaoh in a ceremonial place or a priest acting on his behalf, to ensure divine protection and success for the coming harvest. This act was a reenactment of the mythological plowing of the earth by Geb, the god of the earth, preparing it for Osiris' rebirth and the sprouting of vegetation.

The 'Sowing of the Seed' ritual followed, where offerings of grain were made to Osiris and prayers were recited for a bountiful harvest. The seeds themselves were sometimes mixed with the earth from sacred sites or with water used in temple rituals to imbue them with magical properties and ensure their fertility. The act of sowing was imbued with symbolism, representing the burial of Osiris and his following rebirth, mirroring the cycle of life, death, and regeneration that was central to Egyptian cosmology.

As the crops grew, they were protected by rituals aimed at warding off natural disasters and pests. These included magical spells, the placement of amulets in the fields, and processions of priests who recited hymns and prayers to invoke the protection of the gods. The boundary stones of fields were also anointed with sacred oils and inscribed with protective symbols, further linking the agricultural practice to religious and magical rites. The harvest season brought its own set of rituals, celebrating the reaping of the crops and the collection of the first fruits, which were offered to the gods in gratitude. The 'Harvest Festival' was a time of joy and celebration, marked by feasting, music, and dancing. It was also a time of reflection on the cycle of life and the generosity of the earth and the Nile. The Pharaoh held a symbolic place in the harvest rituals, embodying the living god on earth and ensuring the prosperity of his people through his connection to the divine.

The culmination of the agricultural cycle was the 'Offering of the First Fruits' to the gods, particularly Osiris, as a gesture of thanksgiving and to ensure the continued fertility of the land. These offerings, which included grains, fruits, vegetables, and flowers, were made in temples and were accompanied by prayers and incantations that praised the gods for their bounty and sought their blessings for the coming year.

The rituals of ancient Egyptian agriculture and harvest were a confirmation of the civilization's deep connection to the natural world and their understanding of the interdependence between human activities and the divine. These rituals were not just practical acts aimed at ensuring agricultural success but were also deeply symbolic, reflecting the Egyptians' beliefs in the cyclical nature of life, the power of regeneration, and the presence of the divine in the everyday world. Through these rituals, the ancient Egyptians expressed their gratitude to the gods, celebrated the bounty of the earth, and reaffirmed their place within the universal order, ensuring the continuation of their civilization's prosperity and harmony with the universe.

XI: THE SOLAR BOAT RITUAL AND SUN WORSHIP

The solar boat ritual and sun worship in ancient Egypt stand as monumental testaments to the civilization's religious depth, cosmological understanding, and the profound reverence for the sun as a primary deity. The sun, embodied by the god Ra (or Re), was central to ancient Egyptian theology, symbolizing creation, resurrection, and the cyclical nature of life and the afterlife. The solar boat ritual, intertwined with the worship of the sun, includes the Egyptians' complex beliefs about the sun's adventure across the sky, its passage through the underworld at night, and its triumphant rebirth at dawn, reflecting the eternal cycle of death and regeneration.

Ra, the sun god, was believed to sail across the sky each day in his solar boat, called the "Barque of Millions of Years," and go through the underworld at night to be reborn each morning. This daily adventure was not merely a natural phenomenon but a voyage fraught with danger, as Ra battled the forces of chaos embodied by Apophis, the serpent of darkness and destruction. The solar boat ritual was symbolic of this adventure, embodying the Egyptians' prayers for Ra's victory over chaos, ensuring the sun's return and the maintenance of ma'at, the universal order. The ritual significance of the solar boat is most famously depicted in the discovery of the Solar Boat of Khufu at Giza, near the Great Pyramid. This full-sized, remarkably preserved cedarwood boat, intended for Khufu's use in the afterlife, exemplifies the belief in the necessity of a vessel to navigate the waters of the underworld, mirroring Ra's nightly adventure. The construction and burial of such boats alongside pyramids and tombs were part of the broader funerary rites aimed at providing the deceased with the means to join Ra in his eternal cycle, symbolizing the soul's passage through death and its hope for resurrection and eternal life.

Sun worship in ancient Egypt extended beyond the reverence for Ra and was manifested in various forms and through different deities associated with the sun. The god Amun, merged with Ra to become Amun-Ra, represented the hidden aspect of the sun and its creative force. The cult of Amun-Ra, centered in Thebes, became one of the most powerful in ancient Egypt, reflecting the sun's overarching significance in Egyptian theology and the king's place as the deity's earthly embodiment. The temples dedicated to Amun-Ra, especially the magnificent complex at Karnak, were sites of elaborate rituals and ceremonies celebrating the sun's power and its place in creation and renewal. Another aspect of sun worship was the reverence for the sun disk, Aten, which became the focal point of the monotheistic revolution under Pharaoh Akhenaten. Akhenaten elevated Aten above all other gods, emphasizing the sun disk as the sole source of life and sustenance, a radical departure from traditional Egyptian polytheism. The hymns to Aten, praising its life-giving radiance and universal benevolence, reflect the sun's central place in Egyptian cosmology and the pharaoh's attempt to reframe religious practice around solar worship.

The rituals associated with sun worship were diverse, including daily prayers and offerings at sunrise, the construction of obelisks and sun temples designed to capture the sun's rays, and the celebration of solar festivals. The Sed festival, although primarily a rejuvenation festival for the king, also had solar connotations, symbolizing the renewal of the king's powers in parallel with the solar cycle. Solar festivals celebrated the key points of the sun's adventure, including the winter solstice, which marked the rebirth of the sun, and were occasions for communal rejoicing in the sun's life-giving potency. The symbolism of the sun in ancient Egyptian culture was pervasive, influencing art, architecture, literature, and daily life. The sun was a symbol of divine kingship, with the pharaoh often depicted as the son of Ra, wielding the sun's power on earth. The ubiquitous solar motifs in tomb and temple decorations, including the scarab beetle, which represented the sun's cycle of death and rebirth, and the winged solar disk, a symbol of protection and divine authority, attest to the sun's all-encompassing significance.

The solar boat ritual and sun worship in ancient Egypt were not mere aspects of the civilization's religious practices but were central to its understanding of the universe, the divine, and the condition of humanity. These beliefs and rituals reflect the ancient Egyptians' profound engagement with the natural world, their quest for understanding and control over the forces of chaos, and their hope for eternal life through identification with the sun's unending cycle. The sun, as a symbol of power, creation, and renewal, permeated every aspect of Egyptian religious thought, leaving a lasting heritage that continues to illuminate the depth and complexity of ancient Egyptian civilization. Through their reverence for the sun, the ancient Egyptians expressed their awe before the cosmos, their yearning for order and continuity, and their lasting quest for immortality, themes that vibe through the ages and speak to the universal experience of humanity.

XII: The Place of Music and Dance in Egyptian Rituals

Music and dance in ancient Egyptian rituals were not mere forms of entertainment but essential components of religious and ceremonial practices, deeply intertwined with the civilization's beliefs, cosmology, and the veneration of deities. These art forms were believed to possess the power to communicate with the divine, to effect transformation and to ensure the harmony of the cosmos. Through music and dance, the ancient Egyptians expressed their understanding of the divine order, celebrated the cycles of nature, and sought to influence the world beyond the physical, making these practices central to religious ceremonies, funerary rites, and festivals.

The significance of music in Egyptian rituals is evident from the earliest periods of Egyptian history. Instruments like flutes, harps, lyres, drums, and sistrums (a type of rattle associated with the goddess Hathor) were not just used to accompany religious hymns and chants but were also believed to have magical properties. The sistrum, in particular, was thought to appease the gods, drive away evil spirits, and induce fertility. It was used extensively in rituals dedicated to Hathor, the goddess of music, dance, and fertility, symbolizing the joy and celebration associated with her worship. Music was respected as a living offering to the gods, capable of invoking their presence and favor during rituals and ceremonies. Dance, similarly, was an integral part of Egyptian religious practice, embodying the universal order and the movement of celestial bodies. Dances were performed by both professional dancers, often associated with temples and religious cults, and by participants in religious festivals. These dances could be highly structured and symbolic, enacting mythological narratives, divine attributes, or universal patterns. For example, the ritual dance performed during the Opet Festival, which celebrated the rejuvenation of kingship and the divine essence of the pharaoh, was believed to reenact the creation of the world and the eternal cycle of life and death. Dance, in this context, was not merely symbolic but was seen as a reiteration and reaffirmation of the universal order, a physical manifestation of the principles that governed the universe.

The funerary context highlights another dimension of the place of music and dance in ancient Egyptian rituals. Music accompanied the procession to the tomb and was performed during funerary rites to soothe the deceased and to facilitate their adventure to the afterlife. The "Songs of Isis and Nephthys," chanted by mourning women who emulated the goddesses' lament for Osiris, were believed to aid in the resurrection of the dead, just as Isis' lament had helped to resurrect Osiris. Dance, too, held a place in funerary rites, with the muu-dancers performing at the entrance to the tomb to ward off evil spirits and to guide the deceased safely into the afterlife. These practices underscored the Egyptians' belief in the efficacy of music and dance to bridge the world of the living and the dead, to ensure the deceased's safe passage and acceptance into the world of the gods.

Festivals were another arena where music and dance held a central place, serving both to celebrate the gods and to reinforce social and universal harmony. The Sed Festival, for example, featured music and dance as part of the pharaoh's ritual rejuvenation and the reaffirmation of his divine mandate to rule. The Feast of Hathor, celebrated at Dendera, was marked by ecstatic music and dance, reflecting Hathor's association with joy, fertility, and sensual pleasure. These festivals, through the medium of music and dance, allowed for a communal expression of devotion, joy, and identity, linking the participants with the divine order and with each other in a shared religious experience. The integration of music and dance into Egyptian rituals reflects a holistic understanding of the universe, where the auditory and the kinetic were as necessary as the visual and the spoken in maintaining the balance of the cosmos and ensuring the favor of the gods. These art forms were not adjuncts to religious practice but were fundamental to the Egyptians' interaction with the divine, embodying their beliefs in the power of sound and movement to communicate with the gods, to influence the spiritual world, and to affirm the eternal cycles of nature and the cosmos.

Music and dance in ancient Egyptian rituals were living expressions of religious belief and cosmological understanding, serving as mediums for divine communication, transformation, and the maintenance of universal order. Through these practices, the ancient Egyptians sought to harmonize the human with the divine, the earthly with the celestial, reflecting a civilization that viewed religion and art as inextricably linked facets of the experience of humanity. The lasting heritage of music and dance in Egyptian rituals underscores the profound place these art forms held in articulating and sustaining the spiritual and social map of ancient Egyptian society, offering insights into their worldview, their conception of the divine, and their ceaseless quest for harmony within the cosmos.

XIII: THE USE OF MAGIC AND SPELLS IN ANCIENT EGYPT

The use of magic and spells in ancient Egypt was a fundamental aspect of the civilization's religious and daily life, permeating every facet from the most grandiose temple ceremonies to the most mundane aspects of daily existence. Magic, or heka, was respected as a natural force, a gift from the gods, particularly from Heka, the god of magic, which could be harnessed by humans to influence the world around them, protect against harm, and communicate with the divine. This belief in the power of magic reflects the ancient Egyptians' understanding of the universe as an interconnected whole, where the actions of gods, humans, and the natural world were intimately linked. The use of spells, amulets, and magical rituals was thus not seen as supernatural but as a part of the natural order, essential for maintaining balance and harmony in both the physical and spiritual worlds.

Magic in ancient Egypt was primarily protective and healing in nature, designed to avert danger, cure illnesses, and protect individuals from malevolent forces, including demons, ghosts, and the evil eye. Spells and incantations were used extensively for personal protection, especially in funerary contexts, to safeguard the deceased's adventure through the underworld. The Pyramid Texts, the oldest known religious texts from ancient Egypt, contain spells that were inscribed on the walls of the pyramids to protect the pharaoh in the afterlife and ensure his resurrection and union with the sun god, Ra. These texts illustrate the belief that words, spoken or written, possessed intrinsic power that could be activated through ritual to achieve specific ends. The Coffin Texts and the Book of the Dead, which followed the Pyramid Texts, expanded the availability of magical protection to a broader segment of Egyptian society. These texts included spells to guide and protect the deceased through the dangers of the underworld, to provide knowledge needed to navigate this world, and to ensure a favorable judgment in the Hall of Ma'at. The Book of the Dead, in particular, exemplifies the personalized nature of ancient Egyptian magic, as copies of the book were often customized for the individual, including spells that mirrored their status, concerns, and aspirations for the afterlife. Amulets and talismans were another important aspect of Egyptian magic, embodying spells or invoking the protection of specific deities. These objects were worn in life and death and placed within the wrappings of mummies to ward off evil, promote healing, and confer various benefits on the wearer. The heart scarab, for example, was placed over the heart of the deceased and inscribed with a spell from the Book of the Dead to prevent the heart from betraying the individual during the judgment in the afterlife.

Magical practices also extended to the world of healthcare and healing, with physicians and magicians often being one and the same. Medical papyri contain a blend of practical treatments and magical spells, reflecting the belief that illness could have both natural and supernatural causes. Spells were recited, and magical objects were used alongside herbal remedies and surgical procedures to treat diseases, invoking divine powers to aid in the healing process.

State rituals and temple ceremonies also made extensive use of magic to communicate with the gods, protect the nation, and ensure the fertility of the land and the wellness of the people. The daily temple rituals, involving the offering of food, drink, and incense to the gods, were accompanied by spells to reanimate the statues of the gods, allowing them to partake of the essence of the offerings. These rituals were respected as essential for sustaining the gods and maintaining ma'at, the universal order. The use of magic in ancient Egypt was thus a complex and integral part of the civilization's worldview, a means of accessing and influencing the divine forces that governed the universe. It was a system of knowledge and practice that empowered individuals, protected the community, and ensured the continuation of the universal order. Through the use of spells, amulets, and magical rituals, the ancient Egyptians sought to harness the power of heka to navigate the challenges of life and the afterlife, reflecting a profound understanding of the enmeshment of all aspects of existence and the potential of humanity's agency to affect the world both seen and unseen.

In essence, the practice of magic and the use of spells in ancient Egypt were not merely aspects of religious or superstitious belief but were foundational to the Egyptian understanding of the universe and the human place within it. Magic was a practical and spiritual resource, a tool for personal protection, healing, and communication with the divine, and a necessary element in the rituals that sustained the gods, the state, and the universal order. The opulent corpus of magical texts, the all over use of amulets and talismans, and the integration of magical practices into daily life and state religion all attest to the central place of magic in ancient Egyptian culture, offering insights into the civilization's complex beliefs and their lasting fascination with the power of the unseen.

XIV: THE SIGNIFICANCE OF THE SCARAB BEETLE IN EGYPTIAN CULTURE

The scarab beetle, specifically the dung beetle species Scarabaeus sacer, held profound significance in ancient Egyptian culture, embodying ideas of transformation, rebirth, and the sun's cyclical adventure. This beetle's behavior of rolling dung into balls, from which it later emerges, paralleled the Egyptian observations of the sun's movements and the cycle of life, death, and rebirth. The scarab became a powerful amulet and symbol, representing the forces of creation and regeneration, and was integrated deeply into Egyptian religious practices, art, and daily life.

Central to the scarab's significance was its association with the sun god Ra. The Egyptians observed the scarab beetle rolling its dung ball and saw a metaphor for the sun's path across the sky, as well as the sun's self-renewal each morning. This behavior led to the belief that the scarab beetle was responsible for pushing the sun along its path, ensuring the continuation of the day and the cyclical nature of time itself. Consequently, the scarab symbolized the idea of rebirth and regeneration, mirroring the daily rebirth of the sun at dawn and the eternal cycle of life, death, and afterlife believed to govern human existence. The use of scarab amulets in ancient Egyptian society was all over, with these objects serving as powerful symbols of protection and transformation. Scarab amulets were often inscribed with the names of pharaohs and gods, or with prayers and spells from the Book of the Dead, and were worn by the living or placed among the wrappings of mummies. The heart scarab, in particular, was a key funerary amulet placed over the heart of the deceased. It was inscribed with a spell intended to prevent the heart from confessing sins against the deceased during the Weighing of the Heart ceremony, ensuring safe passage into the afterlife. The heart scarab thus symbolized the rebirth of the individual in the afterlife, protecting the deceased's ba (soul) and ensuring its unification with the ka (spirit), facilitating resurrection alongside the gods. Scarabs were also used as seals, signifying authority and power, and were incorporated into jewelry, commemorative items, and administrative documents. The practice of burying large commemorative scarabs to mark significant events during a pharaoh's reign, like marriage alliances or military victories, highlights the scarab's place in recording and sanctifying historical moments, embedding them within the universal order represented by the beetle's symbolism. The theological significance of the scarab beetle extended beyond its association with the sun. It was also linked to the god Khepri, an aspect of the sun god Ra representing the morning sun and the concept of creation. Khepri's name, which means "he who comes into being," and his depiction as a man with a scarab for a head, or as a scarab beetle itself, emphasized the themes of emergence, creation, and the eternal renewal of life. Khepri's place in the daily rebirth of the sun positioned the scarab as a symbol of the constant renewal of life, the potential for transformation and growth, and the perpetual cycle of the cosmos.

The integration of the scarab beetle into the map of Egyptian cosmology and daily life illustrates the civilization's deep connection to the natural world and its propensity for finding spiritual and symbolic meaning in the behaviors of animals. The scarab's symbolic resonance was multifaceted, encompassing protection, power, regeneration, and the affirmation of life's cyclical nature. Its prevalence in art, religion, and society attests to the scarab's lasting significance in Egyptian culture, offering insight into the ancient Egyptians' worldview, their understanding of the divine, and their quest for eternal life.

In essence, the scarab beetle encapsulated the ancient Egyptians' profound engagement with themes of life, death, and rebirth, serving as a tangible expression of their religious beliefs and their observations of the natural world. Through the symbolism of the scarab, the ancient Egyptians articulated their understanding of the cosmos, the divine order, and the human desire for renewal and continuity beyond death. The heritage of the scarab beetle in Egyptian culture thus stands as a confirmation of the civilization's opulent spiritual and symbolic territory, reflecting its quest to comprehend the mysteries of life and the universe.

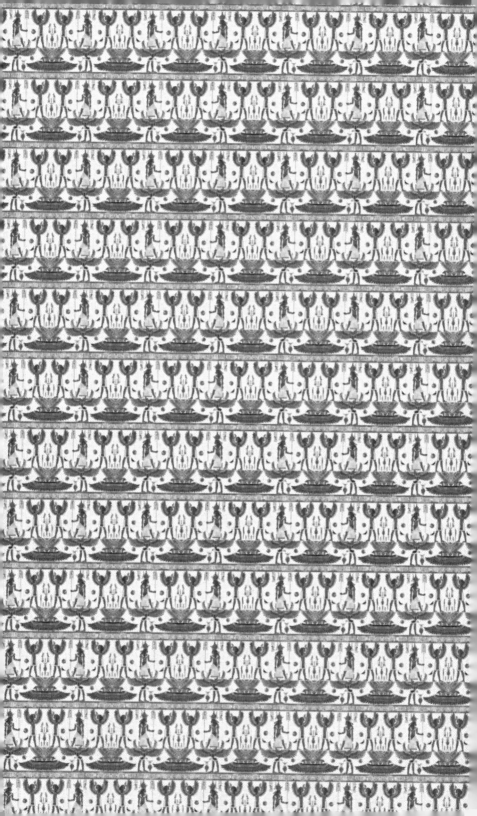

XV: The Mystical Properties of Egyptian Amulets and Talismans

In the opulent atlas of ancient Egyptian culture, amulets and talismans were not mere decorative items but potent symbols imbued with magical and mystical properties. These objects, crafted from a variety of materials including precious stones, metals, faience, and ceramics, served as living components in the Egyptians' spiritual practices, offering protection, healing, and empowerment to their bearers. The belief in the power of these items was grounded in the ancient Egyptian understanding of the universe, where the physical and spiritual worlds were interconnected, and where magic (heka) was a natural force that could be harnessed through the proper rituals and symbols.

Amulets and talismans in ancient Egypt were designed to act specific functions, each with its own symbolic meaning and purpose. These objects were often worn on the body, placed in the wrappings of mummies, or included in the furnishings of tombs, to ensure protection, health, prosperity, and safe passage through the afterlife. The forms these amulets took were diverse, each chosen for its association with particular deities, universal principles, or natural forces, and each believed to confer specific benefits on its wearer.

One of the most famous amulets was the Eye of Horus (Wedjat Eye), symbolizing healing, protection, and restoration. The myth behind this symbol involves the god Horus losing an eye in his battle with Set, only for it to be restored, symbolizing the triumph over chaos and the restoration of wholeness. As an amulet, the Eye of Horus was thought to ward off evil, ensure the health and safety of the bearer, and provide wisdom and prosperity.

The Ankh, representing life and immortality, was another powerful symbol in ancient Egyptian amulets. Its form, resembling a cross with a loop at the top, was believed to stand for the key to the Nile or the breath of life. The Ankh was frequently held by deities in Egyptian art, signifying their ability to bestow life or navigate the afterlife. For the living and the dead, the Ankh served as a potent talisman for protection and the promise of eternal life. The Scarab beetle, symbolizing rebirth and the rising sun, was one of the most popular amuletic symbols in ancient Egypt. The dung beetle, which rolls balls of dung across the ground, was associated with the solar deity Khepri, who rolls the sun across the sky. Scarab amulets were often inscribed with spells or the names of the deceased and placed over the heart of mummies to ensure rebirth and protection in the adventure through the underworld.

Djed pillars, symbolizing stability, endurance, and the god Osiris' backbone, were worn as amulets to ensure the wearer's strength, health, and wellness. The Djed was also a sign of Osiris' resurrection and, as such, represented the hope for eternal life and the sustenance of the soul in the afterlife.

The Tyet, or Knot of Isis, resembling an Ankh with its arms at its sides, was associated with the goddess Isis and her magical powers of protection and healing. The Tyet was believed to offer protection, particularly in funerary contexts, ensuring the safety and wellness of the deceased in the afterlife.

Amulets in the form of deities were also common, with each god or goddess offering their specific protection or blessings. Amulets of Isis were believed to protect children and ensure healing, while those of Bes, a dwarf god, offered protection against evil spirits and were especially popular in households.

The crafting and consecration of these amulets were carried out with great care, involving rituals and spells to activate their magical properties. The materials used were chosen for their symbolic meanings and inherent magical qualities. For example, lapis lazuli, associated with the heavens, was used for amulets that sought to invoke divine protection or favor.

In ancient Egyptian thought, amulets and talismans bridged the mundane and the divine, serving as tangible manifestations of the spiritual forces that governed the universe. They were essential tools for navigating the challenges of life and the afterlife, embodying the ancient Egyptians' desire for protection, health, prosperity, and eternal life. Through these objects, the Egyptians sought to align themselves with the universal order, harnessing the powers of the gods and the natural world to ensure their wellness and spiritual fulfillment.

The mystical properties of Egyptian amulets and talismans reflect a civilization deeply engaged with the spiritual dimensions of existence, where magic was charted into the map of daily life and the afterlife. These objects offer a window into the ancient Egyptians' worldview, their understanding of the divine, and their ceaseless quest for harmony with the forces that shaped their world. Through the study of these amulets and talismans, we gain insight into the complex relationship of religion, magic, and material culture in ancient Egypt, revealing a society that sought to master the mysteries of life and death through the power of heka and the protection of the gods.

XVI: THE CONCEPT OF MA AT AND RITUALS OF ORDER AND JUSTICE

The concept of Ma'at in ancient Egyptian culture represented a foundational principle that was both universal and social, encompassing truth, justice, order, and balance. This concept was personified by the goddess Ma'at, who was depicted wearing an ostrich feather and often presented as a small figure offering the feather of truth. Ma'at's place in the cosmos was to maintain the order established by the creator god at the world's inception, ensuring the universe's continued harmony and preventing the return to chaos. In the societal context, Ma'at represented the ethical and moral principles that governed human behavior, ensuring social harmony and justice within the community. The king or pharaoh, as the earthly embodiment of the divine, was seen as Ma'at's chief upholder, responsible for maintaining universal and social order through rituals, laws, and governance.

The rituals associated with Ma'at were integral to both temple ceremonies and the daily lives of the ancient Egyptians. In the temples, rituals performed by priests on behalf of the pharaoh were aimed at renewing and sustaining the gods, thereby ensuring the maintenance of Ma'at in the cosmos. These rituals included offerings of food, drink, and incense to the gods, which were believed to nourish the deities and appease their needs, thus keeping the forces of chaos at bay. The recitation of hymns and prayers during these rituals invoked Ma'at's principles, seeking the gods' favor and the continued wellness of Egypt and its people.

One of the most significant rituals related to Ma'at was the daily offering ceremony performed in temples across Egypt. This ceremony involved the presentation of offerings to the god's statue within the naos, or sanctuary, which was respected as the god's earthly dwelling place. The ritual symbolized the feeding of the god, ensuring their strength and ability to uphold Ma'at. The offering of Ma'at herself, in the form of a statuette or symbol of the goddess, was a key part of this ritual, symbolizing the reiteration of order and balance in the cosmos.

The Sed festival, a jubilee celebration held in the later years of a pharaoh's reign, was another ritual that underscored the concept of Ma'at. It was designed to rejuvenate the pharaoh's strength and reaffirm his ability to govern in accordance with Ma'at. During the festival, the pharaoh performed a series of rituals and physical challenges that demonstrated his fitness to continue ruling and his alignment with Ma'at. The festival's emphasis on renewal and continuity mirrored the eternal cycle of order, justice, and balance that Ma'at represented. In the world of law and governance, the pharaoh was respected as the primary upholder of Ma'at, responsible for enacting laws and delivering justice in accordance with the principles of truth and balance. The ideal of Ma'at influenced legal decisions and the administration of justice, guiding the resolution of disputes and the punishment of wrongdoing in a manner that sought to restore harmony to the community. Officials and judges were also expected to embody Ma'at in their conduct and decision-making, ensuring that their actions contributed to the maintenance of social order and justice.

The concept of Ma'at also held a necessary place in the afterlife, as seen in the Weighing of the Heart ceremony depicted in the Book of the Dead. In this judgment scene, the deceased's heart was weighed against the feather of Ma'at to determine their worthiness to enter the afterlife. A heart balanced with the feather indicated a life lived in accordance with Ma'at, allowing the deceased to proceed to the Field of Reeds, a paradisiacal world of eternal harmony. This ceremony underscored the belief that adherence to Ma'at's principles in life was essential for a favorable outcome in the afterlife, reflecting the intertwining of universal order, moral conduct, and the fate of the soul.

The all over veneration of Ma'at and the incorporation of her principles into various aspects of Egyptian life underscore the profound significance of this concept in ancient Egyptian culture. Ma'at was not merely an abstract ideal but a practical guide to living that influenced law, governance, religion, and personal ethics. The rituals and practices dedicated to upholding

Ma'at were fundamental to the Egyptians' understanding of the universe, their society, and their place within the universal order. Through the observance of these rituals, the ancient Egyptians sought to align themselves with the forces of order and justice, ensuring the stability of the cosmos and the prosperity of their civilization.

In total, Ma'at represented the ancient Egyptians' aspiration towards harmony, balance, and justice in every aspect of existence, all the way from the universal to the individual level. The rituals and practices associated with Ma'at were expressions of this deep-seated belief in the importance of order and balance, serving as a constant reminder of the enmeshment of all things and the responsibility of each individual to contribute to the maintenance of harmony in the world. Through the concept of Ma'at and the rituals that celebrated and reaffirmed its principles, the ancient Egyptians crafted a vision of the world that was deeply grounded in the values of justice, truth, and balance, offering an eternal example of the pursuit of ethical living and universal harmony.

XVII: THE PROCESSION OF MIN: FERTILITY RITES AND CELEBRATIONS

The Procession of Min was one of the most significant and living fertility rites and celebrations in ancient Egyptian culture, dedicated to Min, the god of fertility, agriculture, and male sexual potency. Min's cult was among the oldest in Egypt, with its origins tracing back to the Predynastic period, and his worship persisted throughout the millennia of Egyptian history. The festival celebrating Min, known for its emphasis on fertility, regeneration, and the renewal of life, was a reflection of the ancient Egyptians' deep connection to the cycles of nature and their reliance on the land's fecundity for survival and prosperity.

Min was typically depicted in anthropomorphic form, holding his erect phallus in one hand and a flail in the other, symbolizing his place as a god of fertility and his association with the sovereign power of the pharaohs. His image was often crowned with feathers and sometimes shown with a head of lettuce, a vegetable believed to possess aphrodisiac qualities, further emphasizing his fertility attributes. The annual festival in honor of Min, which took place during the early harvest season, was not just a time for celebrating fertility and sexuality but also served to ensure the fertility of the land and the wellness of the community.

The Procession of Min was characterized by a series of elaborate rituals and public celebrations, which included music, dancing, and feasting, all aimed at invoking the god's blessings. The highlight of the festival was the grand procession in which the cult image of Min was paraded from the temple out into the fields, symbolizing the god's presence and direct involvement in the blessing of the harvest. This procession was led by the pharaoh or a high-ranking official, underscoring the close association between the king's ritual actions and the fertility and prosperity of the state. The pharaoh's participation in the festival reaffirmed his place as the earthly representative of the divine order and his responsibility for maintaining Ma'at, the universal balance, through the fertility of the land. During the festival, offerings of lettuce and other produce were made to Min, and rituals were performed to ensure the land's fertility and the people's procreative abilities. The lettuce, because of its association with Min and its milky sap suggestive of semen, was a particularly potent symbol of fertility. These offerings were accompanied by prayers and incantations, seeking Min's favor for abundant harvests and the continuation of life through procreation.

Another significant aspect of the Procession of Min was the ritual of "cutting the sheaf," in which the pharaoh ceremonially harvested the first sheaf of grain, dedicating it to Min as a symbolic gesture to ensure the success of the harvest. This act was not just a ritual offering but also a magical act, believed to transfer the god's potency and vitality to the crops, guaranteeing their growth and abundance.

The celebrations associated with the Procession of Min also featured athletic competitions, music, and dancing, reflecting the joy and exuberance associated with the renewal of life. The open expression of sexuality, integral to the festival's fertility theme, was manifested in symbolic acts and rituals that celebrated human and agricultural fertility. These celebrations served to break down the usual social constraints, allowing for a communal expression of gratitude and hope for the future, reinforcing the bonds within the community and with the divine.

The festival's emphasis on fertility, regeneration, and the renewal of life was a reflection of the ancient Egyptians' understanding of the natural world and their place within it. By celebrating Min and invoking his powers, the Egyptians sought to align themselves with the forces of creation and to ensure the continued harmony and balance of the cosmos. The Procession of Min was thus not just a celebration of fertility and life but also an affirmation of the Egyptians' belief in the enmeshment of the divine, the natural world, and human society.

The Procession of Min and the accompanying fertility rites and celebrations were integral to ancient Egyptian religious and social life, embodying the civilization's profound connection to the cycles of nature and their reliance on the divine for sustenance, prosperity, and continuity. Through these rituals, the ancient Egyptians expressed their reverence for the forces of life and fertility, celebrated the generative powers of the earth and the gods, and reaffirmed their place within the universal order. The festival of Min, with its opulent symbolism, rituals, and communal celebrations, offers a vivid window into the spiritual and cultural world of ancient Egypt, highlighting the civilization's lasting fascination with the mysteries of life, fertility, and the eternal cycle of renewal.

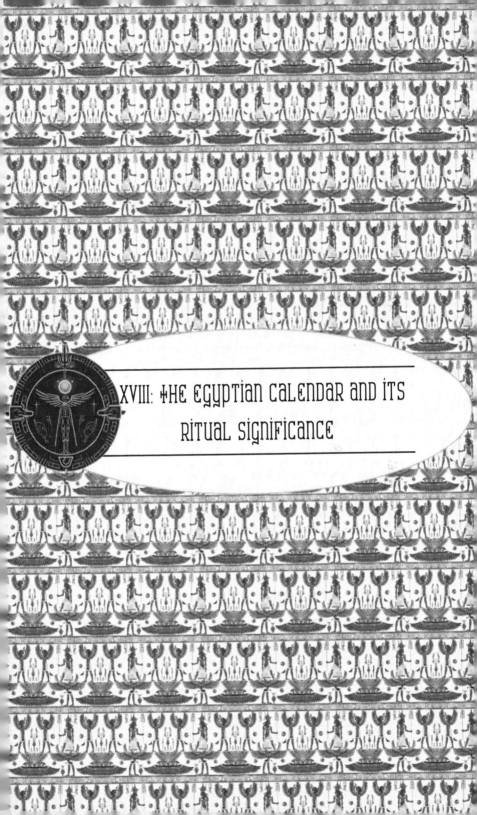

XVIII: THE EGYPTIAN CALENDAR AND ITS RITUAL SIGNIFICANCE

The Egyptian calendar, one of humanity's earliest timekeeping systems, was deeply intertwined with the country's rituals, religious practices, and cosmology, reflecting the ancient Egyptians' sophisticated understanding of astronomy and their keen observation of the natural world. This calendar was not merely a tool for marking time but a sacred schema that aligned human activities with the divine order, ensuring harmony between the heavens and the earth. The ritual significance of the Egyptian calendar was manifested in the timing of religious festivals, agricultural activities, and royal ceremonies, all of which were synchronized with celestial phenomena and the cyclical patterns of nature.

The ancient Egyptian calendar was primarily solar, based on the heliacal rising of Sirius (Sothis), the brightest star in the sky, which coincided with the annual inundation of the Nile River, a critical event that replenished the land's fertility. This calendar consisted of 365 days divided into 12 months of 30 days each, with an additional five epagomenal days at the end of the year, dedicated to the birthdays of the gods Osiris, Horus, Set, Isis, and Nephthys. The reliance on the solar cycle and the observation of Sirius for the calendar's foundation underscored the Egyptians' desire to align their temporal system with universal rhythms and the regenerative powers of nature.

The ritual significance of the Egyptian calendar is perhaps most vividly illustrated in the timing of religious festivals, which were integral to the spiritual and social life of ancient Egypt. These festivals, carefully recorded on temple walls and papyrus texts, were not arbitrary celebrations but were carefully scheduled to coincide with specific astronomical and seasonal markers. For example, the festival of Wepet Renpet, or the New Year, was celebrated with the appearance of Sirius in the morning sky, signaling the Nile's flood and the renewal of the land. This festival was a time of joy and renewal, marked by offerings, processions, and the invocation of blessings for the coming year, reflecting the Egyptians' gratitude for the Nile's life-giving waters and the benevolence of the gods.

Another key festival, the Beautiful Festival of the Valley, was timed to coincide with the full moon during the second month of the season of Shemu, marking a time of connection between the living and the dead. During this festival, processions of the god Amun's image moved across the Nile from Karnak to the west bank of Thebes, visiting the necropolis and reinforcing the bonds between the gods, the pharaoh, and the ancestors. The synchronization of this festival with the lunar cycle underscores the importance of celestial phenomena in determining the timing of religious ceremonies and the ancient

Egyptians' belief in the enmeshment of the universal, terrestrial, and underworld worlds.

The calendar also held a necessary place in agricultural practices, dictating the timing of planting and harvesting based on the seasonal cycles and the Nile's inundation. The beginning of the flooding season, Akhet, marked a period of preparation for the sowing of seeds, while the emergence of the land from the receding waters signaled the start of the growing season, Peret. The harvest season, Shemu, was a time of reaping the benefits of the land's fertility, celebrated with offerings to the gods in gratitude for their bounty. The alignment of agricultural activities with the calendar's cycles was a manifestation of Ma'at, the principle of universal order, ensuring that human endeavors were in harmony with the divine will and the natural world. The Egyptian calendar's ritual significance extended to the coronation of kings and the celebration of their reign through festivals like the Sed festival, which was carefully timed to reinforce the pharaoh's divine mandate and rejuvenate his powers. The precise timing of these ceremonies within the calendar scaffolding underscored the pharaoh's place as the intermediary between the gods and the people, responsible for maintaining universal and social order.

The Egyptian calendar was a sacred construct that infused temporal measurement with profound ritual and cosmological meaning. It was a tool for organizing and sanctifying time, aligning human activities with the rhythms of the universe, and ensuring the continuity of the universal order. Through the calendar, the ancient Egyptians expressed their understanding of time as a cyclical and eternal process, governed by the gods and imbued with ritual significance. The synchronization of religious festivals, agricultural cycles, and royal ceremonies with the calendar's structure reflects the civilization's deep engagement with the divine, the natural world, and the cosmos, revealing a sophisticated worldview that sought harmony between humanity and the broader universe. The ritual significance of the Egyptian calendar thus offers a window into the spiritual and cultural life of ancient Egypt, highlighting the civilization's quest to live in accordance with the principles of Ma'at and to secure the favor of the gods through the careful observation and sanctification of time.

XVIX: THE CULT OF ISIS: RITUALS AND INFLUENCE

The Cult of Isis, dedicated to the worship of the goddess Isis, was one of the most significant and lasting religious movements in ancient Egyptian religion, with its influence spreading throughout the Greco-Roman world. Isis, respected as the goddess of magic, motherhood, fertility, death, and rebirth, was a central figure in Egyptian mythology, embodying the ideals of the devoted wife and mother. Her cult centered on the myth of Isis and Osiris, which told the story of her search for her murdered husband Osiris, the reassembly of his body, and the birth of their son, Horus. This myth encapsulated themes of love, loyalty, resurrection, and the eternal struggle between order and chaos, resonating deeply with the Egyptian people and later with Greek and Roman devotees.

Isis's worship was marked by an opulent atlas of rituals and ceremonies, which evolved over time and varied across different regions. Central to her cult was the emphasis on personal devotion and the promise of protection and salvation, both in this life and the afterlife. The rituals performed in honor of Isis were designed to invoke her power and benevolence, seeking her intervention in matters of health, fertility, and protection. One of the key rituals associated with the Cult of Isis was the annual celebration of the Osiris mysteries, which commemorated the death and resurrection of Osiris. These ceremonies, which included processions, dramatizations of the myth, and offerings, symbolized the cycle of life and death and the hope for renewal. Participants in these rituals sought to identify with Isis's sorrow and joy, experiencing a sense of personal rebirth and spiritual regeneration.

Another important aspect of Isis's worship was the use of magic and spells, believed to have been taught to her by Thoth, the god of wisdom. Isis was respected as the supreme magician, whose knowledge of magic allowed her to resurrect Osiris and protect Horus from harm. Her devotees used spells and amulets invoking her power for protection against dangers and to heal illnesses. The use of such magical practices reinforced the belief in Isis's omnipotence and her place as a protector and healer.

The initiation rites of the Isis cult were another significant element, marking the transition of devotees to higher levels of understanding and closer communion with the goddess. These rites, which remain somewhat mysterious due to the secretive nature of the cult's practices, were believed to involve symbolic death and rebirth, echoing the myth of Osiris. Initiates were sworn to secrecy, and through their participation in these rites, they gained deeper spiritual insights and a personal connection with Isis.

Isis's worship also included daily rituals performed by priests and priestesses in her temples, which involved offerings of food, drink, and incense, as well as the recitation of hymns and prayers. The temples served as centers of healing, with the goddess's power invoked to cure the sick. Pilgrims visited these temples seeking Isis's blessings and protection, offering votive gifts in gratitude for her intervention.

The influence of the Cult of Isis extended beyond Egypt, spreading throughout the Roman Empire and into the Greco-Roman world, where she was worshipped alongside other deities in syncretic cults. In these regions, Isis came to be associated with other goddesses like Demeter, Aphrodite, and Hera, reflecting her universal appeal as a deity embodying the feminine principles of nurturing, protection, and salvation. The lasting popularity of the Cult of Isis can be attributed to its emphasis on personal salvation and the afterlife, its appeal to individuals seeking a personal connection with the divine, and its inclusive nature, welcoming devotees from all walks of life. The cult's rituals and ceremonies provided a means for personal and communal expression of faith, the pursuit of mystical knowledge, and the hope for eternal life under the protection of Isis.

In conclusion, the Cult of Isis stands for a profound aspect of ancient Egyptian religion, characterized by opulent rituals, deep symbolism, and all over influence. The cult's focus on personal devotion, magical protection, and the promise of rebirth and salvation resonated with ancient peoples, allowing it to go beyond its Egyptian origins and become one of the most significant religious movements in the ancient world. Through the worship of Isis, devotees sought to align themselves with the universal order, to navigate the trials of life and death, and to secure a place in the afterlife under the benevolent gaze of the goddess. The heritage of the Cult of Isis, with its emphasis on love, protection, and the hope for renewal, continues to allure scholars and spiritual seekers, offering insights into the religious imagination of the ancient world and the lasting appeal of the divine feminine.

XX: THE RITES OF PASSAGE IN ANCIENT EGYPTIAN SOCIETY

Rites of passage in ancient Egyptian society were deeply embedded in the culture's religious beliefs and practices, marking the transition between key stages of life and the afterlife. These rites were not merely ceremonial but were imbued with symbolic meaning, reflecting the ancient Egyptians' understanding of the cosmos, the divine order, and the condition of humanity. Through rites of passage, individuals were prepared for the challenges of the next life phase, with the community's support, under the protection and guidance of the gods.

One of the earliest rites of passage was the naming ceremony, which took place a few days after birth. Names were of profound significance in ancient Egyptian culture, believed to be integral to an individual's identity and fate. The naming ceremony was, therefore, a necessary ritual that conferred protection on the child, invoking the gods' blessings and ensuring the child's integration into the social and universal order. The chosen name often mirrored desirable qualities, divine associations, or hoped-for destinies, emphasizing the belief in the power of names to influence an individual's life path. Coming-of-age rituals marked another critical transition, preparing young people for adulthood and their roles in society. While specific details of these rites are sparse, it is clear that they involved education in moral, religious, and social responsibilities, reflecting the importance of ma'at (the principle of universal order) in guiding personal conduct. For boys, this might include training in their future profession, especially if they were to follow in their father's footsteps, while girls were prepared for their roles as wives and mothers, essential to family and societal stability.

Marriage was another significant rite of passage, celebrated through rituals that emphasized the union's social, economic, and religious dimensions. Marriages were typically arranged by families and involved contracts that outlined the mutual obligations of the bride and groom, reflecting the practical considerations of these unions. However, love and companionship were also valued, as evidenced by love poetry and the affectionate portrayals of couples in art and literature. The marriage ceremony likely included offerings to Hathor, the goddess of love and beauty, and to Isis, the epitome of marital devotion, seeking their blessings for fertility and harmony.

Death and funerary rites constituted the most elaborate rites of passage, reflecting the ancient Egyptians' beliefs in the afterlife and the soul's immortality. The process of mummification, the adventure of the soul through the Duat (underworld), and the final judgment in the Hall of Ma'at were all framed within a complex ritual process that began at the moment of death and continued until the deceased was safely ensconced in the afterlife. This process included the Opening of the Mouth ceremony, which re-animated the mummy, allowing it to eat, breathe, and speak in the afterlife, and the Weighing of the Heart, where the deceased's heart was weighed against the feather of Ma'at to deter-mine their righteousness and eligibility for the afterlife. These rites underscored the communi-ty's place in ensuring the deceased's successful transition, reflecting a collective responsibility for each individual's eternal fate. Other rites of passage, though less well-documented, would have marked significant moments like initiation into religious or professional guilds, coronation ceremonies for pharaohs, and rites associated with the assumption of official duties or titles. Each of these transitions was accompanied by rituals designed to confer divine favor, ensure the individual's preparedness for their new place, and reaffirm their place within the social and universal order.

In essence, rites of passage in ancient Egyptian society were necessary mechanisms for maintaining the balance between the divine, the natural world, and human society. They provid-ed structure and meaning to the individual's life adventure, from birth to death and beyond, en-suring that each transition was recognized, cele-brated, and sanctified. Through these rites, the ancient Egyptians sought to align themselves with the eternal principles of ma'at, securing the gods' favor and the community's support as they navigated the challenges and opportunities of each new life stage. The rites of passage thus reflect the profound enmeshment of religion, society, and the individual in ancient Egyptian culture, offering insights into the civilization's values, beliefs, and the lasting quest for harmony and immortality.

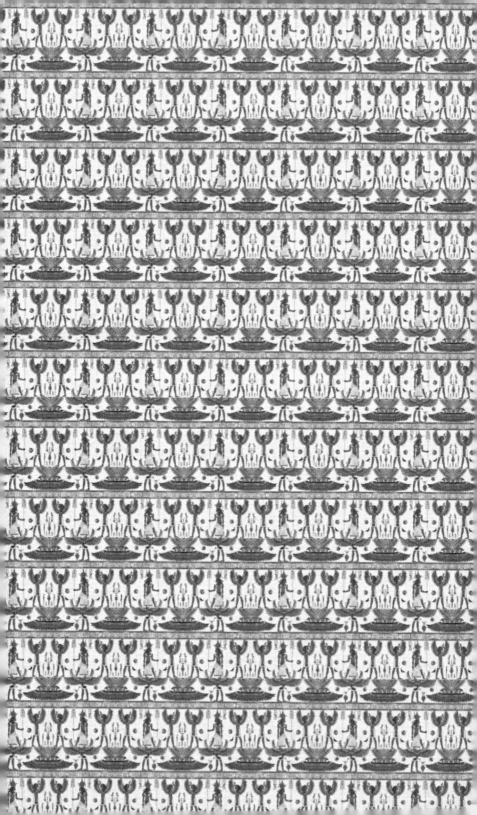

XXI: Symbolism in Egyptian Tomb Paintings and Reliefs

Egyptian tomb paintings and reliefs are a profound confirmation of the civilization's intricate belief system, cosmology, and the importance placed on the afterlife. These artistic creations were not merely decorative but served as symbolic narratives that guided the deceased through the afterlife, ensuring their protection, provision, and resurrection. Embedded within these images are layers of symbolism, each element carefully chosen to reflect the values, aspirations, and religious beliefs of the ancient Egyptians.

The walls of Egyptian tombs were adorned with scenes depicting daily life, religious rituals, mythological narratives, and funerary processes, all intended to ensure a successful transition to the afterlife and eternal wellness. The choice of scenes was deliberate, with each image serving a specific purpose in assisting the soul of the deceased, or "ka," in navigating the afterlife. These paintings and reliefs were essentially magical in nature, believed to become real and functional for the deceased in the afterlife. One of the most prominent symbols found in tomb decorations is the Ankh, representing life and immortality. Often held by gods in tomb paintings, the Ankh signified the divine gift of eternal life and was a common motif in scenes depicting the deceased receiving blessings from deities. Its presence in tomb art was a potent reminder of the life-giving powers of the gods and the hope for life after death.

The depiction of the deceased participating in daily activities like farming, hunting, and feasting served multiple symbolic purposes. These images were not simply reflections of earthly life but were meant to ensure that the deceased would continue to enjoy these activities in the afterlife. By depicting bountiful harvests, successful hunts, and elaborate banquets, the tomb paintings guaranteed that the deceased would have access to food, sustenance, and the pleasures of life, thereby preventing hunger and want in the world of the dead.

Religious rituals and mythological scenes were also central to the symbolism of tomb art. Scenes depicting the adventure of the sun god Ra across the sky, the weighing of the heart ceremony presided over by Osiris, and the protective magic of Isis and Nephthys were common. These images illustrated the deceased's participation in the divine order and their protection by the gods. For example, the depiction of the weighing of the heart against the feather of Ma'at symbolized the judgment the deceased would face and their need to lead a life in accordance with the principles of truth, balance, and moral integrity.

The portrayal of gods and goddesses in tomb paintings and reliefs was highly symbolic, with each deity representing specific aspects of the afterlife and the universal order. For instance, Osiris, often shown presiding over the judgment of the dead, symbolized resurrection and eternal life, while the god Anubis, depicted embalming the deceased or guiding them into the afterlife, represented protection and the transition from death to eternal life. The presence of these deities in tomb art invoked their protection and assistance for the deceased.

Water and boats were recurring motifs in tomb paintings, symbolizing the adventure of the soul to the afterlife. The Nile itself was a symbol of life and fertility, and its depiction in tomb art signified the continuation of life's forces in the afterlife. Scenes of the deceased traveling in boats mirrored the belief in the soul's adventure across the celestial river, mirroring the sun god's nightly adventure through the underworld, a voyage that required divine assistance to navigate successfully.

Color symbolism also held a necessary place in Egyptian tomb art, with each color conveying specific meanings. For example, green represented fertility, growth, and resurrection, while blue symbolized the heavens, water, and primeval creation. The use of these colors was not merely aesthetic but served to invoke the qualities they represented, imbuing the tomb with the powers of regeneration, protection, and divine connection.

Egyptian tomb paintings and reliefs were a visual language that communicated the deceased's desires, beliefs, and their place within the cosmos. These artworks served as a bridge between the earthly and the divine, ensuring the deceased's protection, sustenance, and resurrection in the afterlife. Through the symbolism embedded in these images, the ancient Egyptians expressed their understanding of the universe, the cycles of life and death, and the possibility of eternal life. The tomb art of ancient Egypt thus stands as a confirmation of the civilization's profound spiritual insights, its quest for immortality, and the lasting power of symbolism to convey the deepest aspirations of the human heart.

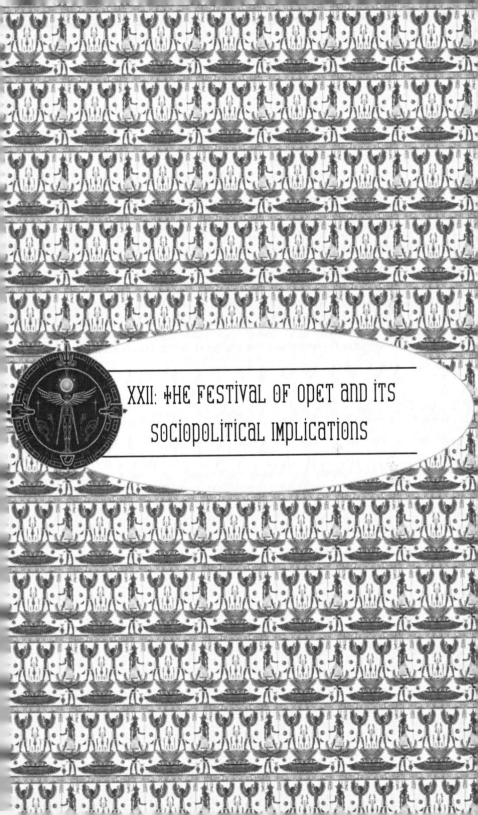

XXII: The Festival of Opet and its Sociopolitical Implications

The Festival of Opet was one of ancient Egypt's most significant religious celebrations, deeply imbued with symbolic meaning and opulent in sociopolitical implications. Held annually in Thebes, the festival centered on the gods Amun, Mut, and Khonsu, whose sacred statues were transported from Karnak to the Luxor Temple along the Nile in a grand procession. This event symbolized the rejuvenation of royal power and the reaffirmation of the pharaoh's divine mandate to rule. The festival, which could last from eleven to almost twenty-four days during the New Kingdom period, was a time of communal celebration, religious devotion, and royal propaganda, reflecting the intricate relationship between religion and politics in ancient Egyptian society.

The procession at the heart of the Opet Festival was a spectacular event, with the statues of the gods carried on barques (sacred boats) from Karnak, the main temple of Amun, to Luxor, where the royal cult was centered. This adventure symbolized the mystical union of Amun and the pharaoh, reinforcing the pharaoh's divine right to rule. The people of Thebes, along with pilgrims from across Egypt, gathered to witness this sacred event, participating in the festivities and receiving blessings from the gods. The procession was not just a religious ceremony but also a public spectacle that demonstrated the wealth, power, and piety of the pharaoh and the state's religious institutions.

The festival's timing, usually occurring during the second month of Akhet, the season of the inundation, was significant. This period marked the Nile's annual flood, which rejuvenated the land and ensured the coming year's agricultural prosperity. The Opet Festival's association with this season underscored the link between the pharaoh's reign, the fertility of the land, and the wellness of the Egyptian people. By aligning the festival with this critical time of renewal, the pharaoh was seen as essential to the universal order, ensuring the country's prosperity through his connection with the gods. One of the most important aspects of the Opet Festival was the ritual of the pharaoh's rejuvenation. During the festival, the pharaoh underwent a series of rituals that symbolically renewed his energies and reaffirmed his fitness to rule. These rites likely included ceremonies of coronation and the presentation of regalia, through which the pharaoh was imbued with the divine essence of Amun. The ritual rejuvenation of the pharaoh served to legitimize his rule, linking his authority directly to the gods and reinforcing the ideology of kingship as a divine institution.

The sociopolitical implications of the Opet Festival were profound. By participating in the festival's rituals, the pharaoh demonstrated his place as both a religious and political leader, responsible for maintaining ma'at, the universal order, through his relationship with the gods. The public nature of the festival allowed the pharaoh to display his power and piety to the populace, reinforcing social hierarchies and the state's central place in religious life. Furthermore, the festival served as an opportunity for the state to distribute food and goods to the people, reinforcing the reciprocal relationship between the ruler and his subjects, where royal generosity and divine favor ensured the people's loyalty and support.

The festival also had significant implications for Thebes's place in Egypt. As the site of the Opet Festival, Thebes was reaffirmed annually as the religious and political heart of the nation, the city where the divine and the earthly worlds intersected. The procession between Karnak and Luxor temples, both significant architectural and religious complexes, underscored the connection between these sites and their central place in the state's ideological and religious territory. In essence, the Festival of Opet was a multifaceted event that encapsulated the complex relationships between religion, politics, and society in ancient Egypt. Through its rituals and ceremonies, the festival celebrated the pharaoh's divine right to rule, reinforced the social order, and underscored the state's place in maintaining the universal balance. The Opet Festival thus served as a powerful tool for legitimizing the pharaoh's authority, encouraging communal identity, and ensuring the continued prosperity and stability of the Egyptian state. Through the lens of the Opet Festival, we gain insight into the ancient Egyptians' worldview, where the divine, the natural, and the political were inextricably linked, and where festivals served as necessary moments of renewal, celebration, and reaffirmation of the social and universal order.

XXIII: THE RITUALS OF ANCIENT EGYPTIAN WARFARE

The rituals of ancient Egyptian warfare were deeply embedded within the religious and cultural map of the society, reflecting the civilization's belief in the divine sanctioning of military endeavors and the integration of the gods into aspects of conflict and conquest. These rituals were not mere formalities but were respected as essential for securing divine favor, protecting the army, and ensuring victory over enemies. Through a combination of prayers, offerings, and symbolic acts, the ancient Egyptians sought to align their military actions with the universal order, invoking the gods' support and legitimizing their campaigns in both defensive and offensive operations.

Before embarking on military campaigns, rituals were conducted to invoke protection and success. Key among these was the consultation of oracles to determine the gods' will regarding the campaign. The decision to go to war was not taken lightly; it required divine endorsement, which was sought through elaborate ceremonies where questions were posed to statues of the gods, which were believed to respond through movements or the uttering of priests. This practice underscored the belief in the gods' active participation in the affairs of state, including warfare, and their ability to guide the pharaoh's decisions.

The blessing of weapons and military standards before battle was another significant ritual. Weapons, seen as extensions of the warrior's body and spirit, were anointed with oils and adorned with protective symbols to imbue them with magical properties. Standards and banners, representing the gods' presence within the army, were also consecrated in ceremonies designed to invoke divine protection and to symbolize the army's righteousness. These rituals reinforced the belief that the army fought with the gods' strength and under their watchful gaze. One of the most important deities in the context of warfare was Montu, the god of war, whose worship was centered in Thebes. Before battles, pharaohs and generals made offerings to Montu, seeking his martial prowess and favor in combat. Montu was often depicted in art and inscriptions as a warrior god, embodying the qualities of valor, strength, and victory that the Egyptians aspired to in their military endeavors. The pharaoh, as the commander of the army, was often equated with Montu, embodying the god's warrior aspect and reinforcing the pharaoh's place as the divine representative on the battlefield.

The place of the pharaoh in the rituals of warfare was paramount. Before military campaigns, the king performed rituals that emphasized his connection to the divine, his place as the protector of Egypt, and his responsibility for maintaining ma'at, the universal order, against the forces of chaos represented by foreign ene-

mies. The Sed festival, although primarily a rejuvenation ceremony for the pharaoh, also had
implications for warfare, symbolizing the renewal of the king's powers, including his martial
abilities, and reaffirming his divine mandate to
rule and protect the land.

Victory in battle was followed by rituals
of thanksgiving and offerings to the gods, ac-
knowledging their place in the triumph. Temples
were significant recipients of the spoils of war,
with part of the booty dedicated to the gods in
gratitude. These offerings not just served to
thank the deities but also to display the
pharaoh's piety and the prosperity his rule
brought to the temple and its god. Triumphal
processions and the erection of victory stelae
were also ritualistic acts, commemorating the
king's success and the gods' favor in a manner
that was designed to be remembered for eternity. The rituals associated with warfare extended
into the treatment of enemies and the dead.
Captured enemies were often presented before
the gods in temples, symbolizing the subjugation
of chaos and the restoration of order. The dead,
both Egyptian and foreign, were subject to rituals that mirrored beliefs about honor, valor, and
the afterlife, underscoring the pervasive influence of religious and universal principles even in
the context of conflict.

The rituals of ancient Egyptian warfare were an integral part of the military strategy, reflecting the civilization's belief in the necessity of divine support for martial success. These rituals demonstrated the Egyptians' view of warfare as an extension of the universal struggle between order and chaos, with the pharaoh and his army serving as agents of the gods to maintain balance in the world. Through these practices, ancient Egyptian warfare was imbued with a level of religious significance that transcended mere physical conflict, integrating the military endeavors into the broader atlas of religious, social, and universal order.

XXIV: THE CULT OF THE APIS BULL AND ITS SYMBOLISM

The Cult of the Apis Bull in ancient Egypt stands as a significant reflection of the civilization's complex religious beliefs and the profound symbolism attributed to animals within their cosmology. The Apis Bull was not merely respected as a sacred animal but was respected as a living manifestation of divine power, specifically associated with Ptah, the god of creation and craftsmanship, and later with Osiris, the god of the afterlife and resurrection. This cult, centered in Memphis, highlights the Egyptians' nuanced understanding of the divine as immanent within the natural world, and the Apis Bull served as a living intermediary between humans and the gods.

The selection of the Apis Bull followed specific criteria, including physical attributes like a black body with a white triangle on the forehead, a scarab mark under the tongue, and double hairs on the tail, among others. These markings were believed to be signs of divine favor, and the discovery of a calf with these characteristics was met with great celebration. The chosen bull was then transported to Memphis, where it lived a life of luxury, housed in a special temple, and attended by priests. The reverence for the Apis Bull was grounded in its symbolic significance, embodying fertility, strength, and virility, and serving as a living talisman for the wellness of Egypt and its people. The worship of the Apis Bull included daily rituals performed by the priests, which involved offerings of food and incense, as well as hymns and prayers. The public was allowed to visit the bull and seek oracles, as it were that the Apis Bull could communicate the will of the gods. On certain occasions, the bull was paraded outside the temple, allowing the populace to partake in its divine presence. These processions were not just religious ceremonies but also public celebrations of the bond between the divine and the earthly worlds, reinforced by the physical presence of the Apis Bull.

The death of an Apis Bull was a moment of national mourning, reflecting the loss of a divine intermediary. The deceased bull was mummified and buried with great ceremony in the Serapeum, a special necropolis near Saqqara. The burial rites mirrored those of the pharaohs, underscoring the Apis Bull's exalted status. The search for a new Apis Bull began immediately, reflecting the continuous cycle of death and rebirth that was central to Egyptian religious thought. This cycle was further symbolized by the association of the deceased Apis Bull with Osiris, whereby the bull was believed to become Osorapis, a fusion of Osiris and the Apis, symbolizing resurrection and eternal life.

The Cult of the Apis Bull also had significant sociopolitical implications, serving as a symbol of the pharaoh's power and legitimacy. The pharaoh was often depicted making offerings to the Apis Bull, highlighting the royal patronage of the cult and the king's place as the mediator between the divine and his people. The association of the bull with both Ptah and Osiris linked the pharaoh with these powerful deities, reinforcing his divine right to rule and his responsibility for maintaining ma'at, the universal order. Over time, the cult gained prominence beyond Egypt, especially during the Ptolemaic and Roman periods, reflecting the adaptability and lasting appeal of Egyptian religious practices. The fusion of the Apis Bull cult with the Greek god Serapis in the Hellenistic period exemplifies the syncretism characteristic of Egyptian religion, as it interacted with and influenced the wider Mediterranean world.

The Cult of the Apis Bull includes the ancient Egyptians' profound reverence for the natural world as a world imbued with divine presence. The Apis Bull, as a living god, embodied the intersection of the celestial and the terrestrial, offering a tangible connection to the divine that could be experienced by both the elite and the common people. Through the rituals and ceremonies dedicated to the Apis Bull, the ancient Egyptians expressed their understanding of the cycles of life and death, the power of renewal, and the presence of the divine in the everyday world. The cult thus stands for a significant aspect of Egyptian religious life, highlighting the civilization's intricate theology, the symbolic importance of animals, and the place of religion in underpinning the social and political order. Through the worship of the Apis Bull, the ancient Egyptians articulated their hopes for fertility, prosperity, and eternal life, underscoring the bull's lasting significance as a symbol of divine power and protection.

XXV: THE PLACE OF PRIESTS AND PRIESTESSES IN EGYPTIAN RITUALS

In ancient Egyptian society, priests and priestesses held a necessary place in the religious and ceremonial life, acting as intermediaries between the divine world and the human world. Their responsibilities were giant and varied, encompassing the performance of rituals, the care of temple deities, the maintenance of sacred knowledge, and the administration of temple estates. The priesthood was not a monolithic institution but a complex hierarchy with various ranks and functions, reflecting the intricate structure of Egyptian religious practices and beliefs.

The core duty of Egyptian priests and priestesses was to act the gods, ensuring that the deities were appropriately worshipped and that their needs were met. This service was performed through daily rituals conducted in the temples, which were respected as the gods' earthly dwellings. The most sacred of these rituals was the daily temple ritual, which involved the awakening, washing, clothing, and feeding of the god's statue. These ceremonies were conducted in the innermost sanctuaries of the temples, accessible only to the highest-ranking priests, and were performed with careful care to adhere to ancient traditions. Through these rituals, the priests and priestesses acted as caretakers of the gods, maintaining the divine presence in the temple and ensuring the continuation of ma'at, the universal order. Priests and priestesses also held a necessary place in the major festivals and processions that punctuated the Egyptian religious calendar. These events, which often involved the transportation of divine statues from one temple to another, required elaborate preparations and rituals to protect the gods and secure their blessings for the people. The priests led these processions, reciting hymns and prayers, performing sacred dances, and making offerings to the gods. These festivals served not just as religious observances but also as public demonstrations of the gods' power and the priests' ability to intercede with the divine on behalf of the people. In addition to their ritual duties, priests and priestesses were custodians of sacred knowledge, including theology, mythology, ritual practices, and magical spells. This knowledge was transmitted through oral traditions and sacred texts, and its preservation was essential for the continuity of religious practices. The priests were often involved in the education of novices and the transmission of esoteric knowledge to initiates, ensuring that the wisdom of the ancients was passed down through generations.

The place of priestesses, while sharing many similarities with that of priests, often had distinct aspects, particularly in temples dedicated to goddesses. Priestesses participated in rituals, music, and dance ceremonies honoring deities like Hathor, Isis, and Bastet. They held living roles in rituals related to fertility, child-birth, and protection, reflecting the association of these goddesses with aspects of women's lives. The divine music and dances performed by priestesses were believed to please the gods and invoke their presence, serving as an essential component of temple worship.

Priests and priestesses also served as intermediaries between the gods and the people, offering guidance, blessings, and divination services. Individuals sought the priests' help for personal matters, including health issues, fertility concerns, and protection against evil forces. The priests used their knowledge of magic and spells to address these concerns, invoking the gods' power to aid their petitioners. This aspect of their place underscored the belief in the gods' immediate presence in the daily lives of the Egyptians and the priests' unique ability to communicate with the divine. The administration of temple estates was another significant aspect of the priesthood's duties. Temples were not just religious centers but also economic powerhouses, owning giant tracts of land, engaging in trade, and employing thousands of workers. The priests were responsible for managing these resources, overseeing agricultural activities, collecting rents, and conducting trade on behalf of the temple. This economic power reinforced the temples' and their priests' influence in ancient Egyptian society, intertwining religious authority with economic and political power.

The priests and priestesses of ancient Egypt were central figures in the religious, social, and economic life of the civilization. Through their service to the gods, they maintained the universal order, ensured the prosperity of the land, and provided spiritual guidance to the people. Their roles mirrored the ancient Egyptians' deep-seated belief in the gods' omnipresence and the necessity of maintaining a harmonious relationship between the divine and the human worlds. The priesthood embodied the interconnection of religion with every aspect of Egyptian life, highlighting the civilization's complex understanding of the divine and the human responsibility in sustaining the balance of the cosmos. Through their rituals, knowledge, and administration, priests and priestesses held a necessary place in the continuity of ancient Egyptian civilization, serving as guardians of its spiritual heritage and as mediators of its sacred traditions.

XXVI: Egyptian Rituals for the Afterlife and Resurrection

The rituals for the afterlife and resurrection in ancient Egypt were founded upon the civilization's profound beliefs in the afterlife, the immortality of the soul, and the possibility of life beyond death. These rituals, which encompassed mummification, tomb construction, funerary rites, and the provision of grave goods, were designed to ensure the deceased's successful transition to the afterlife, their protection and sustenance within it, and ultimately, their resurrection alongside the gods. The complexity and care with which these rituals were performed reflect the Egyptians' deep-seated belief in the afterlife's reality and the importance of maintaining the universal order, or Ma'at, through these practices.

Mummification was among the most critical rituals for the afterlife, embodying the Egyptians' intricate understanding of death and rebirth. This process, aimed at preserving the body against decay, was based on the belief that the physical form was essential for the soul's survival in the afterlife. The embalming process involved the removal of internal organs, dehydration of the body with natron salts, and wrapping in linen bandages. Each step was accompanied by prayers and rituals to purify the body and protect it from evil forces. The heart, respected as the seat of intelligence and emotion, was often left in the body or replaced with a stone scarab inscribed with spells from the Book of the Dead, ensuring the deceased's heart would not testify against them in the afterlife.

The construction of the tomb was another significant ritual, reflecting the belief in the afterlife as a continuation of earthly existence. Tombs were designed as eternal dwellings for the deceased, equipped with all the necessities for the afterlife, including furniture, clothing, and food offerings. The walls were adorned with scenes depicting daily life, religious rituals, and the adventure through the afterlife, serving as magical reinforcements of the deceased's identity and status and guides for the soul's adventure. The tomb was consecrated through rituals that invoked the gods' protection and activated the tomb's magical defenses against malevolent forces. Funerary rites, conducted at the burial and during following visits to the tomb, were essential for commemorating the deceased and maintaining their presence in the afterlife. The Opening of the Mouth ceremony was a necessary ritual, performed to reanimate the deceased's senses, allowing them to breathe, eat, and speak in the afterlife. This ceremony involved the use of special tools to touch the mummy's orifice, symbolically opening them, and was accompanied by spells and offerings to animate the deceased's statue, ensuring their continued existence.

The provision of grave goods, including food, jewelry, amulets, and shabti figurines, was integral to the rituals for the afterlife. These items were believed to become magically available to the deceased in the afterlife, providing protection, sustenance, and assistance with laborious tasks. Amulets, inscribed with spells and worn during life or placed among the mummy wrappings, offered specific protections and powers, like the Djed pillar for stability, the Ankh for life, and the Eye of Horus for health and protection. The recitation of spells from the Book of the Dead and other funerary texts was a necessary aspect of the rituals, guiding the deceased through the dangers of the afterlife and ensuring their successful judgment before Osiris. These spells, inscribed on tomb walls, papyri, and amulets, provided the knowledge and protection needed to navigate the afterlife, overcome challenges, and achieve resurrection.

The rituals for the afterlife and resurrection in ancient Egypt were comprehensive, reflecting a civilization that viewed death not as an end but as a transition to a new existence. Through these practices, the ancient Egyptians sought to ensure the deceased's wellness in the afterlife, maintain their connection to the living world, and secure their eventual resurrection and immortality. These rituals, steeped in religious belief and symbolism, underscore the Egyptians' profound understanding of life, death, and the cosmos, revealing a civilization deeply engaged with the mysteries of existence and the eternal quest for life beyond death.

XXVII: THE USE OF SACRED GEOMETRY IN EGYPTIAN RITUAL SPACES

The use of sacred geometry in Egyptian ritual spaces is a confirmation of the ancient Egyptians' profound understanding of mathematics, cosmology, and their belief in the enmeshment of the physical and spiritual worlds. Sacred geometry, involving the use of symbolic geometric shapes and proportions, was employed in the design and construction of temples, pyramids, and tombs, serving not just aesthetic and functional purposes but also embodying deep symbolic and religious significance. These geometric principles mirrored the Egyptians' desire to align their architectural endeavors with the universal order, harmonizing their ritual spaces with the principles of Ma'at (truth, balance, harmony) and ensuring these spaces were conduits for divine energy and presence.

One of the most significant examples of sacred geometry in ancient Egyptian architecture is the pyramid, particularly the Great Pyramid of Giza. The pyramid's shape, embodying the primordial mound from which the ancient Egyptians believed creation sprang, was a powerful symbol of resurrection and eternal life. The precise alignment of the pyramids with the cardinal points and their proportional relationships, based on the golden ratio and the pi proportion, reflect the Egyptians' sophisticated understanding of geometry and their belief in the importance of celestial alignment. These alignments and proportions were not merely architectural feats but were imbued with religious significance, creating a sacred space that mirrored the heavens, facilitated the pharaoh's ascension to the afterlife, and served as a focal point for solar and stellar cults.

Temples, the dwelling places of the gods on earth, also utilized sacred geometry in their design, reflecting the belief that the physical layout and orientation of these spaces could invoke the divine presence and ensure the efficacy of ritual practices. The axial alignment of temples along the Nile, and with specific celestial bodies, created a direct link between the deity, the temple, and the cosmos, reinforcing the temple's place as a microcosm of the universe. The use of symmetry and harmonic proportions in temple architecture, including the careful placement of columns, pylons, and sanctuaries, was aimed at creating a harmonious and balanced environment that mirrored the order of the cosmos and facilitated the flow of divine energy. The layout of temple complexes often followed a symbolic adventure from chaos to order, mirroring the path of spiritual initiation and the soul's adventure through the afterlife. The progression from the outer courts (symbolizing the chaotic world) to the inner sanctum (the divine world) was a physical and spiritual adventure, guided by the sacred geometry of the space. This adventure was further emphasized by the use of sacred measurements and proportions, which encoded esoteric knowledge and connected the worshipper with the divine.

The use of sacred pools and gardens within temple complexes also reflects the application of sacred geometry, symbolizing the primordial waters of creation and the idealized order of the cosmos. These elements were carefully integrated into the temple's overall design, using geometric principles to create spaces that mirrored the Egyptians' cosmological beliefs and the enmeshment of all life.

In tombs, sacred geometry was employed to ensure the deceased's successful transition to the afterlife and their resurrection. The orientation of tombs, the geometric layout of burial chambers, and the use of specific proportions in the design of sarcophagi and canopic chests were intended to align these spaces with universal forces and protect the deceased. The incorporation of texts and images within these geometrically defined spaces further activated their symbolic power, creating a harmonious environment conducive to the deceased's rebirth. The use of sacred geometry in Egyptian ritual spaces was a manifestation of the ancient Egyptians' desire to integrate the physical and spiritual worlds, to embody the universal order in their architectural endeavors, and to create spaces that facilitated divine encounters and ensured the continuity of life beyond death. Through their sophisticated application of geometric principles, the Egyptians encoded deep religious and cosmological beliefs into their ritual spaces, making these structures not just architectural marvels but also profound expressions of their worldview. The heritage of sacred geometry in Egyptian ritual spaces underscores the civilization's lasting fascination with the mysteries of the universe, the search for harmony and balance, and the quest for transcendence and immortality.

XXVIII: astronomy and astrology in egyptian rituals

The influence of astronomy and astrology in ancient Egyptian rituals underscores the civilization's profound engagement with the cosmos and its belief in the enmeshment of celestial phenomena with terrestrial life. Ancient Egyptians observed the night sky with reverence, recognizing in its patterns both the order of the cosmos and the divine will. This celestial order, embodied in the movements of stars, planets, and celestial events, was not merely a subject of curiosity but a living aspect of religious practices, informing rituals, temple orientations, and the very foundation of the Egyptian calendar.

Astronomy, the observation and study of celestial bodies, held a necessary place in the formulation of the ancient Egyptian calendar, which was essential for regulating religious festivals and agricultural activities. The calendar was based on the lunar and solar cycles, with the heliacal rising of Sirius (Sothis) marking the start of the inundation of the Nile and the new year. This event was of profound ritual significance, heralding a period of renewal and fertility, celebrated with offerings and prayers to the gods. The alignment of temples and pyramids with celestial phenomena, like solstices and equinoxes, further illustrates the importance of astronomy in ritual practices. These alignments ensured that the sacred spaces were in harmony with universal rhythms, enhancing their sanctity and efficacy in religious ceremonies. Astrology, the interpretation of celestial phenomena as signs influencing or reflecting earthly events, was also integral to Egyptian religious thought. While not astrology in the modern sense, the Egyptians believed that the gods communicated through the stars and planets, and that celestial events could portend significant occurrences on earth. The decans, a system of star groups that rose consecutively on the horizon throughout the year, were used for timekeeping during the night and held a necessary place in magical and religious texts, providing a celestial scaffolding for rituals and spells.

One of the most significant celestial phenomena in Egyptian ritual life was the myth of the sun god Ra's daily adventure across the sky and through the underworld. This myth, which depicted the sun's death at sunset and rebirth at dawn, was reenacted in daily temple rituals, with the offering of prayers and hymns to Ra at dawn, noon, and sunset. Solar eclipses and the sun's seasonal variations were interpreted as manifestations of Ra's struggle with the forces of chaos, reinforcing the need for ritual practices to support the sun god's renewal and the maintenance of universal order.

The stars also held profound significance in Egyptian rituals, particularly those associated with the afterlife. The imperishable stars, which never set and were thought to reside in the northern sky, were identified with the souls of the deceased, who became part of the celestial world. The orientation of the Great Pyramid and certain tomb shafts towards specific stars or constellations, like Orion (associated with Osiris) and Sirius (associated with Isis), was intended to facilitate the deceased's ascent to the heavens, ensuring their immortality and union with the divine. The phases of the moon were another aspect of celestial phenomena that influenced Egyptian rituals, particularly those related to fertility, birth, and rebirth. The lunar cycle, with its pattern of waxing, fullness, and waning, was seen as a symbol of regeneration and was incorporated into rituals to harness its life-generating powers. Lunar festivals, like those dedicated to Khonsu, the god of the moon, celebrated the moon's influence on fertility and growth, reflecting the belief in the moon's power to affect the natural and human worlds.

The influence of astronomy and astrology in ancient Egyptian rituals reflects the civilization's holistic view of the universe, where celestial phenomena were not mere occurrences but expressions of divine will and integral components of the universal order. Through their sophisticated observations of the heavens and the incorporation of celestial patterns into their religious practices, the ancient Egyptians sought to align themselves with the rhythms of the cosmos, ensuring harmony between the gods, the natural world, and human society. The integration of astronomy and astrology into Egyptian rituals underscores the civilization's quest for understanding, order, and transcendence, revealing a profound connection between the earthly and the celestial that permeated every aspect of their religious and cultural life.

XXIX: THE PLACE OF WOMEN IN EGYPTIAN RELIGIOUS PRACTICES

The place of women in ancient Egyptian religious practices was multifaceted and integral, reflecting their importance within both the societal and divine worlds. Women engaged in religious activities as deities, priestesses, and worshippers, playing necessary roles that spanned the spectrum of religious life in ancient Egypt. Their participation and influence underscored the balanced approach of the ancient Egyptians to gender roles within religious contexts, recognizing the living contributions of both men and women to the spiritual and ritualistic map of their society.

At the divine level, goddesses held positions of immense power and were central to the religious and mythological narratives of ancient Egypt. Deities like Isis, Hathor, Nut, and Ma'at were venerated for their attributes and responsibilities, which included protection, motherhood, creation, and the maintenance of universal order. Isis, in particular, was respected for her magical prowess, her place as the devoted wife and mother, and her association with resurrection and the afterlife. The all over worship of goddesses demonstrated the recognition of feminine qualities as essential aspects of the divine, influencing how women's roles were perceived and enacted within religious practices. Priestesses served in temples across Egypt, performing a variety of functions that were living to the worship of the gods and the administration of religious institutions. While the roles of priest-esses often paralleled those of their male coun-terparts, certain positions and duties were unique to women. For instance, the place of the God's Wife of Amun, a position of high status within the priesthood of Amun at Thebes, was a religious and political office held by a woman, usually a daughter or wife of the pharaoh. The God's Wife performed important ritual duties, managed significant economic resources, and held a key place in the religious and political life of the state. Other priestesses participated in rit-uals through music and dance, serving as chantresses or musicians, invoking the gods' presence, and facilitating communication be-tween the divine and the worshippers.

Women's participation in religious festi-vals and processions was another avenue through which they engaged with the divine. These public celebrations allowed women to ex-press their devotion, interact with the divine, and seek blessings for themselves and their fam-ilies. The Festival of Opet and the Beautiful Feast of the Valley are examples of such occasions where women, alongside men, participated in processions, made offerings, and celebrated the gods' benevolence. These festivals not just rein-forced social cohesion but also highlighted the communal aspect of religious worship, in which women held active and visible roles.

In the world of personal piety, women engaged in private worship and magic, utilizing spells, amulets, and rituals to protect their homes and families, ensure successful childbirth, and invoke the gods' favor in daily matters. The use of magical objects, like protective amulets worn during pregnancy or childbirth, underscores the practical aspects of women's religious practices, aimed at harnessing divine power for personal and familial wellness. The tombs and funerary practices of ancient Egypt also uncover the importance of women in religious rituals associated with death and the afterlife. Women mourned the dead, participated in funerary processions, and performed rituals to aid the deceased's adventure to the afterlife. The professional mourners, often women, emulated the roles of the goddesses Isis and Nephthys in the Osirian myth, dramatizing the themes of loss, mourning, and the hope for resurrection. These practices highlighted the belief in the intercessionary power of women, both divine and mortal, in the most critical juncture of the experience of humanity— the transition from life to death.

And so, the place of women in ancient Egyptian religious practices was comprehensive, spanning the spectrum from the divine to the mundane. Women's contributions as deities, priestesses, and worshippers were essential to the articulation and maintenance of the religious and cosmological ideals of ancient Egypt. Their active participation in religious life underscored the ancient Egyptians' recognition of the balance between masculine and feminine principles, reflecting a society in which women held living roles in sustaining the spiritual, social, and familial order. Through their engagement in religious practices, women in ancient Egypt exercised agency, influence, and power, contributing profoundly to the religious and cultural heritage of one of history's most fascinating civilizations.

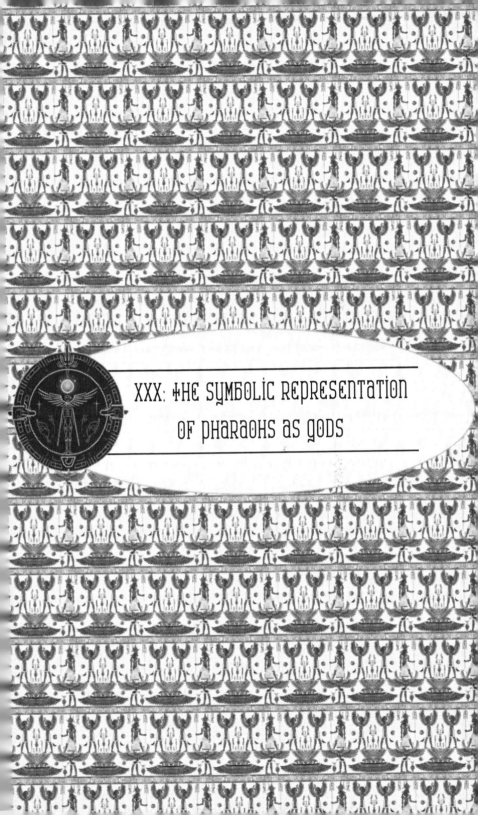

XXX: THE SYMBOLIC REPRESENTATION OF PHARAOHS AS GODS

The symbolic representation of pharaohs as gods within ancient Egyptian culture was a fundamental aspect of the civilization's religious and political scaffolding, reflecting a profound intertwining of divine authority and royal power. This conflation of the pharaoh with the divine world was not merely a tool of statecraft but a deeply ingrained element of Egyptian cosmology, affirming the pharaoh's place as the intermediary between the gods and humanity, the guarantor of ma'at (universal order), and the protector of the nation's welfare. The divinity of the pharaoh was articulated through a complex system of symbols, rituals, and titles that elevated the king above the world of the ordinary, situating him within the pantheon of Egyptian deities and legitimizing his rule through divine sanction. From the earliest periods of Egyptian history, the pharaoh was associated with Horus, the falcon-headed sky god who embodied kingship, power, and protection. The living pharaoh was respected as the "Horus on Earth," embodying Horus's divine authority and serving as the protector of Egypt. This identification with Horus was reinforced through coronation rituals, where the pharaoh received the symbols of Horus's power, including the pschent crown, which unified Upper and Lower Egypt. The pharaoh's place as the earthly manifestation of Horus was further emphasized in royal iconography, with the pharaoh often depicted with the falcon's wings or wearing the falcon's head, symbolizing his divine nature and his protective place over the nation.

The pharaoh's divine status was also expressed through his association with Ra, the sun god, emphasizing the king's place as the son of Ra and the embodiment of solar power. This association highlighted the pharaoh's function as the bringer of light, order, and fertility, mirroring the sun's daily adventure across the sky and its life-giving force. The ritual of the Sed festival, celebrated after thirty years of a pharaoh's reign and periodically thereafter, was a key moment in reaffirming the king's vitality and his continued ability to uphold ma'at. The festival's rituals symbolically rejuvenated the pharaoh's powers, ensuring his equivalence with the eternally youthful and powerful sun god.

Upon death, the pharaoh was identified with Osiris, the god of the afterlife and resurrection. This association underscored the belief in the pharaoh's immortality and his place in maintaining the universal order beyond his earthly reign. The burial practices, including mummification and tomb construction, were designed to facilitate the pharaoh's transformation into Osiris, ensuring his resurrection and eternal life among the gods. The tombs themselves, especially the pyramids, were symbolic representations of the pharaoh's ascension to the heavens, serving as both a physical and spiritual conduit to the divine world.

The divine nature of the pharaoh was communicated to the populace through monumental architecture, statuary, and the proliferation of temple reliefs depicting the king performing rituals or being embraced by the gods. These images served both a religious and propagandistic function, reinforcing the pharaoh's divine status and his necessary place in the religious life of the nation. The temples, as the dwelling places of the gods on earth, were also the setting for the daily rituals that affirmed the pharaoh's place as the high priest of every deity, further blurring the lines between the royal and the divine.

The concept of divine kingship in ancient Egypt was thus a multifaceted and deeply symbolic construct that permeated every aspect of Egyptian religious, political, and social life. The pharaoh's divinity was not a static attribute but a dynamic force, continually reaffirmed through rituals, symbolism, and the active participation of the king in the religious ceremonies of the state. This system of divine kingship served to legitimize the pharaoh's rule, ensuring the stability and continuity of the nation by aligning the king's authority with the immutable order of the cosmos.

Essentially, the symbolic representation of pharaohs as gods was a profound expression of ancient Egyptian cosmology, reflecting a civilization where the bounds between the human and the divine were fluid and interconnected. Through this system, the pharaohs were able to wield immense religious and political power, embodying the principles of ma'at and securing the nation's prosperity and harmony. The divinization of the pharaoh was a central pillar of ancient Egyptian religion and government, illustrating the unique way in which the civilization conceptualized the place of the king, the nature of the divine, and the structure of the cosmos.

XXXI: RITUALS SURROUNDING THE EGYPTIAN CONCEPT OF THE SOUL

The ancient Egyptian concept of the soul was intricate, comprising several components that mirrored the civilization's nuanced understanding of existence, both in the mortal world and the afterlife. Central to this concept were the ka, ba, and akh, among other elements, each representing different aspects of the individual's identity and spiritual essence. The rituals surrounding these soul components were designed to ensure their protection, nourishment, and eventual reunification in the afterlife, facilitating the deceased's transformation into an akh, a blessed spirit capable of eternal existence. These practices were deeply embedded in Egyptian religious beliefs and were manifested in funerary customs, tomb architecture, and the texts that adorned burial sites.

The ka represented the life force or living essence given to a person at birth. Rituals to sustain the ka involved offerings of food, drink, and other necessities, believed to provide sustenance for the ka after death. Temples and tomb chapels often included offering tables and depicted scenes of offerings being presented to the deceased, symbolizing the perpetual care the ka required. The opening of the mouth ceremony, a necessary rite performed during the burial process, was intended to reanimate the deceased's body and statue, enabling the ka to receive these offerings and interact with the physical world.

The ba, often depicted as a human-headed bird, symbolized the individual's personality and mobility. It were to fly between the tomb and the world of the living, maintaining a connection between the deceased and their loved ones. Rituals for the ba focused on ensuring its freedom to move and its eventual reunion with the body, a critical aspect of the individual's resurrection and transformation into an akh. Tombs were constructed with "false doors" and "serdabs" (statue chambers), architectural elements that provided access points for the ba, allowing it to re-enter the tomb and reunite with the ka and the deceased's body.

The akh, representing the transfigured spirit that achieved immortality among the stars, was the ultimate goal of the soul's adventure. Achieving akh status required the successful integration of the ba and ka and the individual's justification in the judgment of Osiris, where the heart was weighed against the feather of Ma'at. The spells and vignettes from the Book of the Dead and other funerary texts were critical to this process, providing the knowledge and protection necessary for the deceased to navigate the underworld, face the judgment, and emerge victorious. These texts, inscribed on tomb walls, papyri, and amulets, were not merely decorative but served as magical aids that activated the tomb's protective functions and guided the soul through the afterlife's challenges.

The rituals surrounding the concept of the soul extended to the community and the living, reflecting the belief in the ongoing relationship between the deceased and their family. The cult of the dead, which involved regular offerings and commemorative feasts at the tomb, served to maintain this connection, ensuring the deceased's wellness in the afterlife and, in turn, securing their intercession on behalf of the living. This practice reinforced the continuity of existence beyond death and the mutual dependencies between the worlds of the living and the dead. The rituals surrounding the Egyptian concept of the soul were comprehensive, addressing the needs and challenges faced by the ka, ba, and akh. These practices mirrored a sophisticated theological scaffolding that integrated aspects of magic, morality, and cosmology, underscoring the ancient Egyptians' deep engagement with the mysteries of life, death, and the afterlife. Through these rituals, the Egyptians sought to ensure the eternal wellness of the soul, facilitating its adventure towards immortality and its transformation into an akh. This system of beliefs and practices underscores the civilization's profound understanding of the spiritual dimensions of existence, revealing a culture that viewed death not as an end but as a complex transition to a new form of life. The rituals surrounding the soul thus provide a window into the ancient Egyptians' worldview, highlighting their quest for eternal existence and their belief in the lasting power of the soul.

XXXII: THE EFFECT OF FOREIGN CULTURES ON EGYPTIAN RITUAL PRACTICES

The ancient Egyptian civilization, with its opulent atlas of rituals and religious practices, was not isolated from the influences of neighboring cultures. Throughout its history, Egypt engaged in extensive trade, military conquests, and diplomatic relations with other civilizations, leading to the assimilation and adaptation of foreign religious practices and deities into its own ritualistic scaffolding. This cross-cultural exchange was a confirmation of the dynamism and adaptability of Egyptian religious practices, reflecting the civilization's ability to integrate new ideas while maintaining the core principles of its own beliefs.

One of the most significant impacts of foreign cultures on Egyptian ritual practices was the introduction and incorporation of new deities into the Egyptian pantheon. Gods like Astarte and Baal from the Levant, and Isis and Osiris's worship in the Greco-Roman world, are prime examples of how Egyptian religion absorbed foreign elements. Astarte, a goddess of war and fertility, was assimilated into the Egyptian pantheon during the New Kingdom, reflecting the interactions between Egypt and the Levantine cultures through trade and military campaigns. Similarly, the worship of Isis extended far beyond Egypt's borders, becoming a major cult in the Roman Empire. The adaptability of Isis's cult, which emphasized universal themes of protection, magic, and salvation, facilitated its acceptance in diverse cultural settings, illustrating the reciprocal influence between Egyptian and foreign religious practices. The effect of foreign cultures was also evident in the adoption and adaptation of new ritual practices and symbols. For instance, the introduction of horse-drawn chariots and composite bows from the Near East during the Second Intermediate Period and the New Kingdom transformed military rituals and the representation of the pharaoh as a warrior deity. The incorporation of these technologies not just changed the practical aspects of warfare but also influenced the symbolic repertoire of royal power and divine protection, as demonstrated in temple reliefs and royal tombs.

The Hyksos occupation of the Delta region during the Second Intermediate Period introduced new religious practices and deities, like the storm god Set, who was initially venerated by the Hyksos and later integrated into the Egyptian pantheon as a major deity. This period of foreign rule, while initially disruptive, ultimately contributed to the enrichment of Egyptian religious and ritual practices, demonstrating the complex relationship between cultural exchange and religious adaptation.

The Ptolemaic period, marked by Greek rule in Egypt, was another era of significant cross-cultural exchange. The Greek rulers adopted and participated in Egyptian religious practices, while also introducing elements of Greek religion and administration. The cult of Serapis, a syncretic deity combining aspects of Osiris and the bull god Apis with Greek deities like Hades and Dionysus, exemplifies the fusion of Egyptian and Greek religious practices. The construction of the Serapeum in Alexandria, alongside traditional temples, underscored the coexistence of Egyptian and Greek religious traditions and the mutual influences that shaped ritual practices during this period.

The Roman occupation further diversified the religious territory of Egypt, introducing Roman deities and practices into the existing religious scaffolding. However, the lasting strength of Egyptian religious traditions was evident in the continued reverence for ancient deities and rituals, even as Roman emperors participated in Egyptian ceremonies and offered patronage to Egyptian temples. The cult of Isis, in particular, flourished during the Roman period, with temples dedicated to the goddess found throughout the Roman Empire, showcasing the all over influence of Egyptian religious practices beyond its borders.

The effect of foreign cultures on Egyptian ritual practices reveals a civilization characterized by religious openness, adaptability, and the capacity for integration. The assimilation of foreign deities, symbols, and rituals into the Egyptian religious scaffolding did not diminish the distinctiveness of Egyptian beliefs but rather enriched its religious and cultural expression. This dynamic process of cultural exchange and adaptation underscores the enmeshment of ancient civilizations and the fluid bounds between religious traditions. Through the lens of Egyptian ritual practices, we gain insight into the complex relationship between continuity and change, tradition and innovation, and the lasting power of religion to bridge diverse cultures and histories.

XXXIII: THE MYSTERIES OF THE SPHINX: SYMBOLISM AND SPECULATION

The Great Sphinx of Giza, a monumental figure with the body of a lion and the head of a human, has stood as a sentinel over the Giza Plateau for millennia, embodying the mysteries and lasting fascination of ancient Egypt. While not directly tied to the liturgical practices of Egyptian rituals in a manner similar to temple worship or funerary rites, the Sphinx holds a unique place in Egypt's symbolic and speculative territory. Its origins, purpose, and the identity of the pharaoh whose visage it may bear are subjects of ongoing debate and interest, reflecting the complexities of interpreting the past through both archaeological evidence and the lens of ancient symbolism. The Sphinx is traditionally associated with King Khafre (c. 2558–2532 BCE), who ruled during the Fourth Dynasty of the Old Kingdom and under whose auspices the second of the Great Pyramids at Giza was constructed. This association is primarily based on the Sphinx's proximity to the Pyramid of Khafre and the architectural and stylistic elements of the surrounding complex, including the causeway and the Valley Temple linked to Khafre's mortuary complex. The Sphinx faces east, towards the rising sun, a positioning that is emblematic of its place as a guardian of the plateau and its alignment with solar symbolism, a key aspect of ancient Egyptian religious belief.

The symbolism of the Sphinx, with its leonine body and human head, is opulent in meanings and interpretations. The lion was a symbol of royal power, strength, and protection, while the human head is believed to stand for the pharaoh himself, embodying the qualities of intelligence, authority, and divine rule. This amalgamation of humanity's and animal forms captures the essence of pharaonic power, bridging the terrestrial and celestial worlds, and asserting the pharaoh's place as both a temporal ruler and a divine intermediary. The Sphinx, therefore, stands not merely as a work of monumental art but as a symbol of the unity of the king's dual roles, guarding the sacred necropolis and ensuring the perpetuation of universal order, or Ma'at.

Speculation about the Sphinx's deeper meanings and origins has flourished throughout the centuries, fueled by its enigmatic nature and the erosion of contextual information over time. Various theories have been proposed regarding its construction date, with some scholars and alternative theorists suggesting a much earlier origin than traditionally accepted. These speculations often draw on geological studies of erosion patterns, astronomical alignments, and comparisons with other ancient structures, positing that the Sphinx may predate Egypt's Fourth Dynasty and have originally been conceived for a different purpose entirely. The Sphinx's place in ancient Egyptian ritual and religious life, while not explicitly documented in surviving texts from the Old Kingdom, can be inferred from its symbolic attributes and the religious beliefs of the time. It may have served as an apotropaic symbol, warding off evil and protecting the sacred spaces of the Giza Plateau. Its alignment with the sun and the horizon also suggests a connection to solar worship, particularly the cult of Ra, and its embodiment of the horizon (Akhet), where the sun rises and sets, symbolizing rebirth and renewal.

Over the millennia, the Sphinx has accrued additional layers of meaning and speculation. In the New Kingdom, it was respected as Horemakhet ("Horus in the Horizon"), further solidifying its association with solar symbolism and the god Horus. In later periods, including the Greco-Roman era, it was linked with the god Harmachis and became the subject of various legends, including those involving oracles and hidden chambers. The lasting mystery of the Sphinx and its speculative interpretations highlight the challenges of reconstructing ancient beliefs and practices from the archaeological and textual record. The Sphinx stands as a confirmation of the complexity of ancient Egyptian civilization, its religious symbolism, and the perennial human fascination with the unknown. Its silent gaze continues to invite reflection on the nature of divinity, kingship, and the quest for understanding that transcends historical epochs, making it not just a monument of stone but a symbol of the lasting quest for knowledge and the mysteries that lie at the heart of humanity's civilization.

XXXIV: Animal Mummification and its Symbolic Meaning

The practice of animal mummification in ancient Egypt was a complex phenomenon that intertwined religious beliefs, rituals, and symbolism, reflecting the civilization's intricate relationship with the animal world. This practice, which spanned thousands of years, served multiple purposes: from acts of devotion to specific deities, through to expressions of religious piety, and as a means of ensuring the presence of sacred animals in the afterlife. Animal mummification was not merely a reflection of the Egyptians' love for animals but was deeply embedded in the symbolic and religious map of their society, highlighting the place of animals as avatars for deities, symbols of divine protection, and mediators between the human and divine worlds.

Animals were mummified for a variety of reasons and were chosen either because they were respected as sacred to specific deities or because they were beloved pets. Sacred animals, like falcons associated with Horus, ibises with Thoth, and cats with Bastet, were mummified as votive offerings, intended to convey prayers and requests to the gods. The belief was that by mummifying the animal associated with a particular deity, the devotee could gain favor or communicate more directly with that god or goddess. Temples dedicated to these deities often had giant animal necropolises nearby, where thousands of mummified animals were buried, serving as tangible expressions of devotion and piety. The process of mummification for animals mirrored that of humans, albeit on a different scale depending on the animal's size and the resources available to those commissioning the mummification. It involved the removal of internal organs, desiccation of the body with natron salts, and wrapping in linen. Sometimes, the animal bodies were adorned with painted coffins or death masks, further emphasizing their sacred and ceremonial significance. This careful treatment underscored the belief in the sanctity of these animals and their place in religious rituals and the afterlife.

Pets were also mummified, reflecting the emotional bonds between Egyptians and their animals, as well as beliefs about the afterlife where owners hoped to be reunited with their animal companions. Dogs, cats, monkeys, and gazelles are among the pets that were mummified, indicating the range of animals that were kept and cherished in ancient Egyptian households. The mummification of pets not just spoke to the Egyptians' love for their animals but also to their belief in an afterlife where all creation could be reborn.

Symbolically, animal mummification represented the Egyptians' view of the natural world as imbued with divine presence. Animals were seen as manifestations of the gods on earth, each embodying specific attributes of the deities they represented. For instance, the fierce lioness represented the warrior aspect of the goddess Sekhmet, while the humble dung beetle, or scarab, symbolized the sun god Ra's self-renewal. By mummifying these animals, the Egyptians sought to honor the gods and secure their protection and favor. This practice also mirrored the Egyptians' belief in the enmeshment of all life and the cosmos, where humans, animals, and deities were part of a unified whole. The symbolic meaning of animal mummification extended into the world of the afterlife, where these mummified animals served as guides, protectors, and companions for the deceased. Sacred animals were believed to intercede with the gods on behalf of the deceased or to provide them with the attributes of the gods they represented. Pets, on the other hand, were mummified as beloved companions who could continue to provide comfort and companionship in the afterlife, reinforcing the lasting bonds between humans and animals.

The practice of animal mummification in ancient Egypt was a multifaceted phenomenon that encapsulated the civilization's religious beliefs, emotional life, and cosmological vision. Through this practice, the ancient Egyptians expressed their reverence for the divine, their understanding of the natural world as a world filled with symbolic meaning, and their hopes for eternal life beyond death. Animal mummification, therefore, was not just a ritual practice but a profound expression of the ancient Egyptians' worldview, highlighting their deep connection to the animal world and its significance within their religious and symbolic universe.

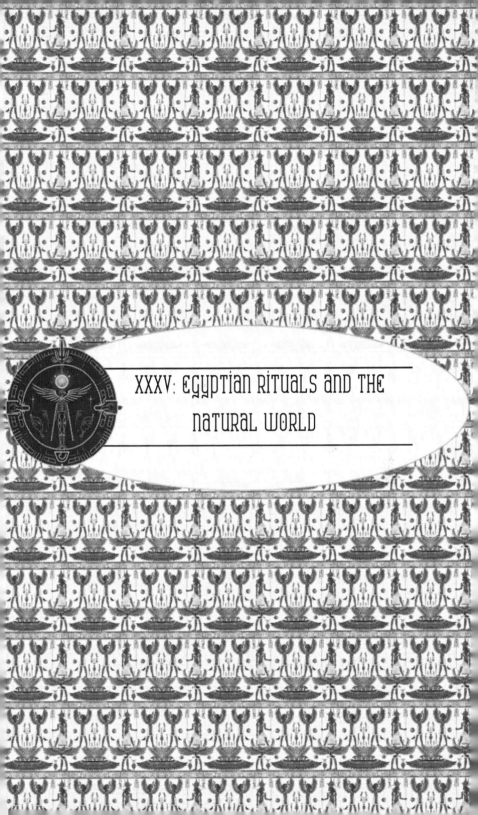

XXXV: Egyptian Rituals and the Natural World

The connection between Egyptian rituals and the natural world is a reflection of ancient Egypt's profound engagement with its environment, where the rhythms of nature were intertwined with religious practices, beliefs, and daily life. This deep-seated relationship was grounded in the Egyptians' observations of the world around them, all the way from the life-giving floods of the Nile to the cycles of the sun and the stars, all of which were imbued with divine significance. The natural world, in all its facets, was seen not merely as a backdrop for human activity but as a manifestation of the gods' work and will. Consequently, Egyptian rituals, whether aimed at ensuring the fertility of the land, honoring the gods, or securing a favorable adventure through the afterlife, were replete with references to, and incorporations of, natural phenomena.

The Nile River, the source of Egypt's fertility and prosperity, was central to Egyptian religious thought and ritual practice. The annual inundation of the Nile, which deposited nutrient-opulent silt along its banks, was celebrated through rituals that expressed gratitude to the gods, particularly Hapi, the god of the inundation. The Wepet Renpet festival, marking the New Year, was closely tied to the Nile's flooding, symbolizing renewal and rebirth. Rituals performed at this time included the offering of first fruits, prayers for continued fertility, and the enactment of scenes depicting the mythological origins of the Nile's bounty. The river's cyclical flooding was seen as a divine gift, essential for agriculture and the survival of Egypt itself, and rituals associated with it were designed to ensure the continuation of this living cycle. The sun, a dominant force in the Egyptian natural and religious territory, was venerated through rituals that acknowledged its power to create life, dictate the passage of time, and illuminate the path to the afterlife. The god Ra, the sun deity, was central to Egyptian cosmology, and his daily adventure across the sky was mirrored in the rituals performed in temples across Egypt. Morning rituals greeted the sun at dawn, offerings were made at noon when the sun's power was at its zenith, and prayers were recited at sunset as the sun descended into the underworld. Solar festivals, like the Feast of Opet, celebrated the rejuvenating power of the sun and its association with the pharaoh, the "son of Ra," whose coronation and regnal anniversaries were often timed to coincide with significant solar events.

The natural world also featured prominently in funerary rituals and beliefs about the afterlife. The adventure of the deceased through the underworld was fraught with challenges that mirrored the perils and uncertainties of the natural world. Rituals performed for the dead, including the Opening of the Mouth ceremony and the provision of grave goods, were intended to equip the deceased with the means to navigate this adventure, invoking the protection of deities associated with natural phenomena, like the sky goddess Nut and the earth god Geb. The Book of the Dead, a compilation of spells and incantations, contains numerous references to natural elements, employing them as metaphors for spiritual transformation and rebirth. Agricultural rituals further underscored the connection between Egyptian religious practices and the natural world. Festivals celebrating the harvest and the sowing of seeds were occasions for communal gatherings, where offerings were made to ensure the fertility of the land and the success of the crops. These rituals acknowledged the gods' place in providing for the people and sought to align human activities with the divine order, ensuring harmony between the heavens, the earth, and the underworld.

The connection between Egyptian rituals and the natural world reflects a civilization that viewed itself as an integral part of a divinely ordered cosmos. Every aspect of the natural world, all the way from the Nile River and the sun to the flora and fauna that flourished in Egypt, was infused with symbolic meaning and incorporated into the religious practices of the people. Through these rituals, the ancient Egyptians expressed their gratitude to the gods, sought to maintain the balance of Ma'at, and navigated the cycles of life, death, and the afterlife, always with an eye to the natural world that sustained and surrounded them. This profound connection to nature, charted into the map of Egyptian religious and ritual practices, highlights the civilization's lasting heritage as a culture that found divinity in the natural world and sought harmony with its rhythms and cycles.

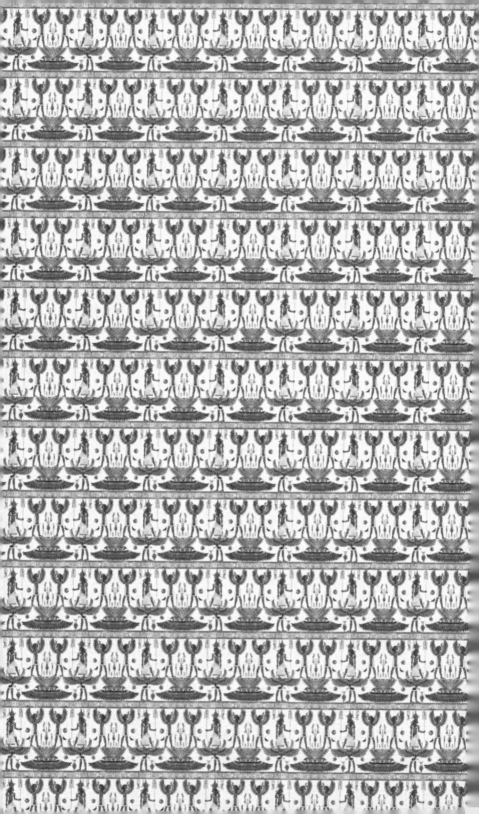

XXXVI: THE PLACE OF DREAMS AND VISIONS IN EGYPTIAN SPIRITUALITY

In ancient Egyptian spirituality, dreams and visions were not merely ephemeral experiences but were imbued with profound significance, serving as living conduits for divine communication, personal revelation, and prophetic insight. The Egyptians recognized dreams as a means through which the gods conveyed messages to the living, offering guidance, warnings, and wisdom. This belief in the spiritual and symbolic importance of dreams is evident in various texts, tomb inscriptions, and religious documents, underscoring the place of dreams and visions as integral components of Egyptian religious and cultural life.

Dreams were respected as a form of divine interaction, wherein the bounds between the earthly and the divine worlds were permeable. The gods, it were, could enter an individual's dreams to deliver messages or to offer protection and support. This perspective is mirrored in the numerous accounts of dream encounters with deities found in Egyptian literature, like the Story of Sinuhe and the Instructions of Amenemope, where dreams act as necessary moments of divine intervention and personal transformation.

The significance of dreams extended to the world of the pharaohs, who were respected as the gods' earthly representatives. Royal dreams were particularly auspicious, often seen as omens concerning the welfare of the state or as divine endorsement of royal policies and actions. One notable example is found in the Dream Stele of Thutmose IV, which recounts how the sphinx, representing the sun god Horemakhet, appeared to Thutmose in a dream, promising him kingship in return for clearing away the sand that engulfed the Sphinx. This dream was not just a legitimizing force for Thutmose's rule but also underscored the belief in the protective and beneficent place of the gods in the affairs of state, communicated through the medium of dreams.

The interpretation of dreams was a specialized practice, with certain priests and scribes acting as dream interpreters or "masters of the secret things." These individuals possessed the knowledge to decipher the symbolic language of dreams, translating the divine messages contained within them. The Dream Book (or Chester Beatty Papyrus) is a prime example of an ancient dream manual, listing various dream scenarios and their meanings, which ranged from predictions of prosperity and success to warnings of impending danger or misfortune. This text illustrates the Egyptians' attempt to categorize and understand the dream world's complexities, reflecting a systematic approach to dream interpretation that acknowledged the dream world's significance in everyday life and decision-making.

Dreams also held a necessary place in personal spirituality and religious practices. Individuals sought dreams as a form of personal revelation, undertaking rituals and sleeping in sacred spaces, like temples dedicated to specific deities, to induce divine dreams. These "incubation" rituals were believed to facilitate direct communication with the divine, allowing the seeker to receive guidance, healing, or knowledge. The practice underscores the proactive place individuals could take in seeking divine interaction, highlighting the personal dimension of Egyptian spirituality.

In the context of the afterlife, dreams and visions were intertwined with beliefs about the soul's adventure and the transformation of the deceased. Visions experienced by the living, relating to the deceased or the afterlife, were seen as significant, offering reassurance about the loved ones' wellness in the afterlife or providing insight into the spiritual world. Such experiences reinforced the continuity between life and death and the enmeshment of the living, the dead, and the divine.

Dreams and visions in ancient Egyptian spirituality were multifaceted phenomena that bridged the human and divine, offering insight, guidance, and reassurance. They were vehicles for divine communication, integral to personal and state religiosity, and reflective of the Egyptians' broader cosmological views. Through dreams and visions, the ancient Egyptians navigated the complexities of their world, seeking understanding and connection with the divine forces that shaped their existence. This reverence for the dream world underscores the profound spiritual depth of Egyptian culture, where the seen and unseen, the known and the mysterious, were inextricably linked in the quest for wisdom, protection, and eternal life.

XXXVII: THE SYMBOLISM OF THE LOTUS FLOWER IN EGYPTIAN CULTURE

The lotus flower, with its striking beauty emerging from the murky waters of the Nile, held profound symbolic significance in ancient Egyptian culture, encapsulating themes of creation, rebirth, and the sun's daily adventure. This symbolism permeated various aspects of Egyptian religious beliefs, rituals, and artistic expressions, making the lotus not merely a common motif in Egyptian art and mythology but a potent symbol of the enmeshment of life, death, and rebirth, as well as the cyclical nature of the cosmos. Central to the lotus flower's symbolism was its association with the sun and creation. Each morning, the lotus blooms with the first rays of the sun, only to close and sink beneath the water at night, mirroring the sun's adventure across the sky and its nightly passage through the underworld. This daily cycle made the lotus a natural emblem of the sun's rebirth at dawn, symbolizing the triumph of light over darkness, life over death. In this context, the lotus was often linked with the sun god Ra, reinforcing the deity's place in creation and the renewal of life. Depictions of the sun god rising from a lotus blossom were common, illustrating the belief in the flower as the source of divine creation and the eternal renewal of the universe.

The lotus flower was also emblematic of rebirth and regeneration in the context of the afterlife, a belief that was integral to Egyptian funerary practices and mythology. The Book of the Dead, which contains spells and incantations designed to guide the deceased through the afterlife, frequently references the lotus in contexts that underscore its place in resurrection and eternal life. The deceased were often depicted holding lotus flowers, symbolizing their hope for rebirth and renewal in the afterlife, akin to the sun's daily rebirth. Tombs and sarcophagi featured lotus motifs, serving as magical symbols to protect and rejuvenate the soul of the departed. Also, the lotus was closely associated with the concept of purity and the divine. The flower's ability to emerge unspoiled from the muddy waters of the Nile was seen as a metaphor for the purity and perfection of the spiritual world, untainted by the chaos and impurity of the physical world. Deities, particularly those associated with creation and beauty, like Nefertum and Hathor, were often depicted with lotus flowers, highlighting their purity, divine beauty, and place in the universal order. The offering of lotus flowers to the gods in temple rituals was a common practice, symbolizing the devotee's desire for purification and divine favor.

The lotus also symbolized the unity and duality of life, embodying the balance and harmony of the universe. Its blue and white varieties represented Upper and Lower Egypt, respectively, reflecting the country's unification and the pharaoh's place as the ruler of a unified nation. The flower's symmetry and the harmonious arrangement of its petals evoked Ma'at, the principle of universal order and balance, further embedding the lotus within the map of Egyptian cosmology and royal ideology. In the world of personal adornment and daily life, the lotus motif was prevalent in jewelry, amulets, and household objects, serving not just as a decorative element but also as a talisman for protection, fertility, and rebirth. The pervasive presence of the lotus in everyday items underscored its significance in the collective consciousness of the ancient Egyptians, permeating every aspect of their lives with its symbolic meanings.

In essence, the symbolism of the lotus flower in Egyptian culture was a multifaceted reflection of the civilization's religious beliefs, cosmological views, and values. The lotus encapsulated the ancient Egyptians' observations of the natural world and their interpretation of these observations within a religious and mythological scaffolding. Through the symbolism of the lotus, the Egyptians expressed their understanding of life's cyclical nature, the relationship of chaos and order, and the possibility of renewal and rebirth. The lotus thus stands as a confirmation of the depth and complexity of Egyptian symbolism, embodying the eternal quest for understanding, purity, and harmony with the cosmos.

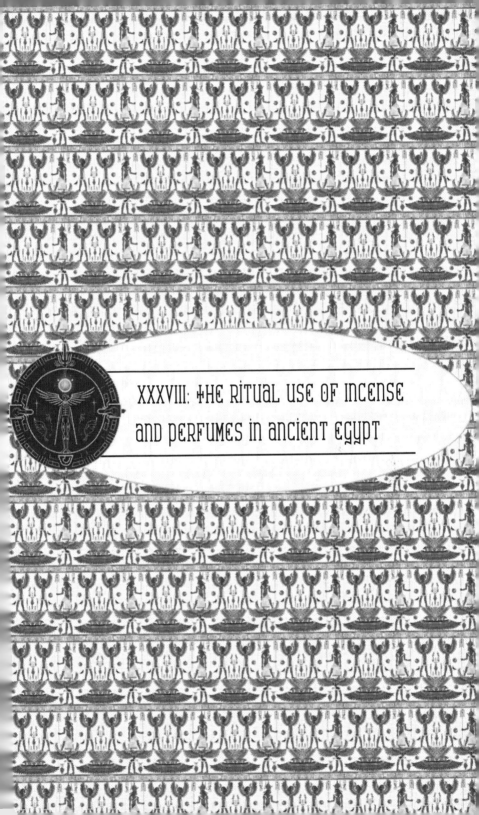

XXXVIII: THE RITUAL USE OF INCENSE AND PERFUMES IN ANCIENT EGYPT

The ritual use of incense and perfumes in ancient Egypt was an integral aspect of their religious practices, deeply embedded in the spiritual, cultural, and daily life of the civilization. These aromatic substances were not merely used for their pleasant fragrances but were imbued with profound symbolic meanings, serving as mediums for purification, communication with the divine, and the embodiment of prayers and blessings. The use of incense and perfumes was pervasive, spanning temple rituals, funerary practices, and personal adornment, reflecting the ancient Egyptians' sophisticated understanding of the olfactory power to invoke the sacred, protect against malevolent forces, and ensure harmony with the universal order.

In temple rituals, incense and perfumes held a necessary place in the daily offerings made to the gods. The burning of incense, particularly kyphi (kapet), a complex blend of natural ingredients, including resins, herbs, and spices, was a central act of worship. The act of burning incense was symbolic of the transformation of tangible offerings into ethereal smoke, which carried the prayers and invocations of the priests upward to the divine world. The smoke's ascent was seen as a visual representation of the connection between earth and heaven, with the pleasing aroma acting as a means to appease the gods, invite their presence, and ensure their favor. Incense was also used to purify the temple space, cleansing it of impurities and creating an environment conducive to divine encounters.

Perfumes, made from a wide array of aromatic oils and substances, were used in both religious rituals and personal grooming. In a religious context, perfumes were applied to the statues of deities as part of the ritual of divine adornment, symbolizing the consecration of the god's image and the impartation of life force. Perfumed oils were also used in the mummification process, serving both practical purposes of preservation and symbolic functions of regeneration and rebirth. The use of perfumes in mummification echoed the broader Egyptian belief in the power of aromatic substances to facilitate the transition to the afterlife and the deceased's transformation into a divine being. The funerary context further underscores the ritual significance of incense and perfumes. Tombs were stocked with jars and containers of aromatic substances, ensuring the deceased's continued access to these materials in the afterlife. Incense was burned during funerary rites to purify the deceased and the mourners, ward off evil spirits, and guide the soul on its adventure to the afterlife. The pleasant aromas were believed to be pleasing to the gods who would judge the deceased, making incense an essential offering for securing a favorable outcome in the afterlife.

Beyond their use in formal religious and funerary contexts, incense and perfumes permeated daily life, reflecting the ancient Egyptians' desire for cleanliness, beauty, and protection. Perfumed oils were used extensively for personal grooming, not just for their pleasant scents but also for their cooling and moisturizing properties in Egypt's arid climate. The wearing of perfumes was believed to bring the wearer under the protection of the gods, with different scents associated with specific deities and their attributes. Incense was burned in homes to purify the space, repel insects, and create an atmosphere of sanctity and wellness.

The ritual use of incense and perfumes in ancient Egypt, therefore, was a multifaceted practice that transcended the mere sensory pleasure of fragrance. It was a symbolic act that engaged the divine, facilitated spiritual transformation, and expressed the ancient Egyptians' desire for purity, protection, and communion with the gods. Through the burning of incense and the application of perfumes, the Egyptians sought to harmonize their environment with the universal order, ensuring the flow of ma'at (balance, truth, and order) in both the physical and spiritual worlds. These practices highlight the civilization's deep connection to the natural world, their understanding of the material as a conduit to the divine, and the integral place of sensory experience in their religious and cultural expressions.

XXXIX: THE PRACTICE OF DIVINATION AND ORACLES IN EGYPTIAN RELIGION

The practice of divination and oracles in ancient Egyptian religion was a complex and integral part of the civilization's quest to understand the will of the gods and to secure guidance for both mundane and significant matters. Divination, the attempt to gain insight into questions or situations through ritualistic practices or observations, and oracles, responses from the gods to these inquiries, were deeply embedded in Egyptian religious and social life. These practices underscored the Egyptians' belief in a cosmos where the divine and the human worlds were interconnected, and where the gods actively communicated their will to the people. Divination in ancient Egypt took various forms, ranging from the interpretation of dreams and the examination of natural phenomena, to the use of specific objects or rituals designed to elicit divine responses. Dream interpretation was particularly significant, as dreams were respected as a medium through which the gods could directly communicate with individuals. Specialized priests, known as "masters of the secret things" or "learned ones of the magical library," often performed the interpretation of dreams, translating the symbolic language of the gods into guidance for the dreamer. This practice was so integral to Egyptian culture that manuals for dream interpretation, like the Chester Beatty Papyrus, were produced, listing common dream motifs and their meanings.

Another method of divination involved the observation of natural phenomena, like the behavior of animals or the flight of birds, which were interpreted as omens. The Nile's annual flooding was also closely watched, with its levels believed to indicate the gods' favor or displeasure, thereby influencing agricultural practices and temple offerings. These forms of divination were part of a broader attempt to read the signs provided by the natural world, which was seen as imbued with divine significance.

Oracles held a necessary place in the decision-making processes of the state and individuals alike. Temples often served as centers for oracular consultation, where the god's statue would be asked questions, and the responses would be interpreted by priests. One notable method involved processions where statues of deities were carried and their movements observed for indications of a "yes" or "no" answer to the questions posed by petitioners. This practice was especially prevalent in matters of national importance, like the planning of military campaigns or the appointment of officials, underscoring the belief in the gods' direct involvement in the affairs of the state.

The use of oracles was not limited to the elite; ordinary Egyptians also sought divine guidance in personal matters, including health, fertility, and legal disputes. Temples dedicated to specific deities, like Amun at Karnak, became renowned for their oracular powers, attracting petitioners from across the country. The responses from these oracles were respected as infallible and carried significant weight in both personal and public decision-making, reflecting the deep trust in the gods' wisdom and justice. The practice of divination and oracles also extended into funerary beliefs and practices, where the deceased's fate in the afterlife could be revealed through oracular pronouncements. Funerary texts, like the Book of the Dead, contain spells and incantations intended to aid the deceased in navigating the afterlife, underscoring the belief in the possibility of divine intervention and guidance beyond death.

The practice of divination and oracles in ancient Egyptian religion was a confirmation of the civilization's profound spirituality and its belief in a world where human and divine worlds were closely linked. Through these practices, the ancient Egyptians sought to align their actions with the will of the gods, to ensure harmony and balance in both their personal lives and the cosmos at large. Divination and oracles provided a means of accessing divine wisdom, offering comfort and guidance in the face of uncertainty, and reinforcing the societal and universal order. These practices highlight the Egyptians' desire for knowledge, their reverence for the gods, and their lasting quest to understand the mysteries of existence.

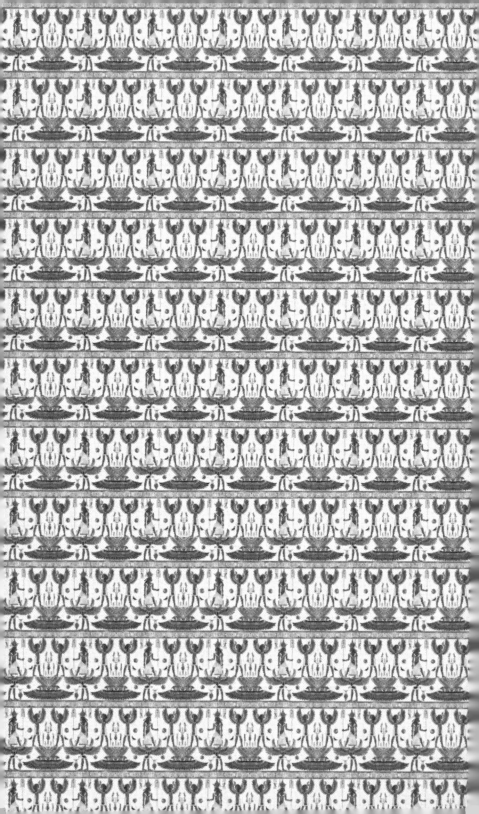

XL: THE SYMBOLISM IN ROYAL REGALIA AND CROWNS

The symbolism embedded in the royal regalia and crowns of ancient Egypt is a profound confirmation of the civilization's complex belief system, intertwining notions of divinity, kingship, and universal order. These items were not merely ornamental but were laden with symbolic meanings, reinforcing the pharaoh's place as the intermediary between the gods and the people, and as the upholder of Ma'at—the fundamental principle of truth, balance, and universal order. Each element of the royal attire, all the way from the crowns and headdresses to scepters, jewelry, and ceremonial garments, was imbued with specific symbolic significance, reflecting the multifaceted nature of the pharaoh's duties and powers.

The crowns of ancient Egypt are particularly emblematic of the pharaoh's authority and divine mandate. The most famous are the Deshret (Red Crown) of Lower Egypt, the Hedjet (White Crown) of Upper Egypt, and the Pschent (Double Crown), which combined the two to symbolize the unification of the country under a single ruler. The Deshret, associated with the red-hued lands of the Nile Delta, symbolized the fertility of the land and the pharaoh's place in ensuring the prosperity of his world. The Hedjet, on the other hand, represented the pharaoh's sovereignty over the giant and arid regions of Upper Egypt, emphasizing themes of purity, spiritual illumination, and divine connection. The Pschent, as a fusion of these two crowns, was a powerful symbol of the pharaoh's ability to unify and govern the dual aspects of the kingdom, embodying the fusion of physical and metaphysical worlds. Another significant crown was the Khepresh (Blue Crown), often worn in battle or during triumphal ceremonies. Its blue hue was associated with the sky and the primeval waters of creation, symbolizing the pharaoh's place as the earthly embodiment of the god of creation and his capacity to bring chaos into order. The Uraeus, a rearing cobra often featured on the brow of royal headdresses, symbolized the sovereign's protection by the goddess Wadjet, embodying divine authority, sovereignty, and the pharaoh's place as the protector of Egypt.

The royal scepter, known as the "heka" (crook) and the "nekhakha" (flail), were symbols of the pharaoh's pastoral place as the shepherd of his people and his capacity to both nurture and discipline. The crook represented kingship, leadership, and the pharaoh's responsibility for his subjects' welfare, while the flail was associated with fertility, the harvest, and the pharaoh's power to ensure abundance.

Jewelry, including necklaces, bracelets, and pectorals, were also laden with symbolism. For instance, the Menat necklace, often associated with the goddess Hathor, symbolized joy, fertility, and protection, and was thought to bring favor from the goddess. Similarly, the Scarab beetle, frequently depicted in royal jewelry, symbolized rebirth, regeneration, and the solar cycle, reinforcing the connection between the pharaoh and the sun god Ra. The royal kilt, known as the "shendyt," was another essential component of the pharaoh's regalia, symbolizing his earthly dominion and his place as the bringer of Ma'at. The ceremonial beard, often braided and made of metal or other materials, denoted the pharaoh's divine knowledge and authority, linking him with the gods.

The symbolism in royal regalia and crowns in ancient Egyptian culture was a multidimensional expression of the pharaoh's divine and earthly roles. Through these symbols, the pharaoh was depicted as the supreme ruler, protector, unifier, and high priest, embodying the qualities necessary to maintain the universal order and ensure the prosperity of his world. The regalia served as visual representations of the pharaoh's power, his connection to the divine, and his responsibility for upholding the principles of Ma'at. In this way, the royal attire of ancient Egypt was not just a reflection of status and power but also a complex language of symbols that articulated the civilization's deepest religious beliefs and its understanding of the universe.

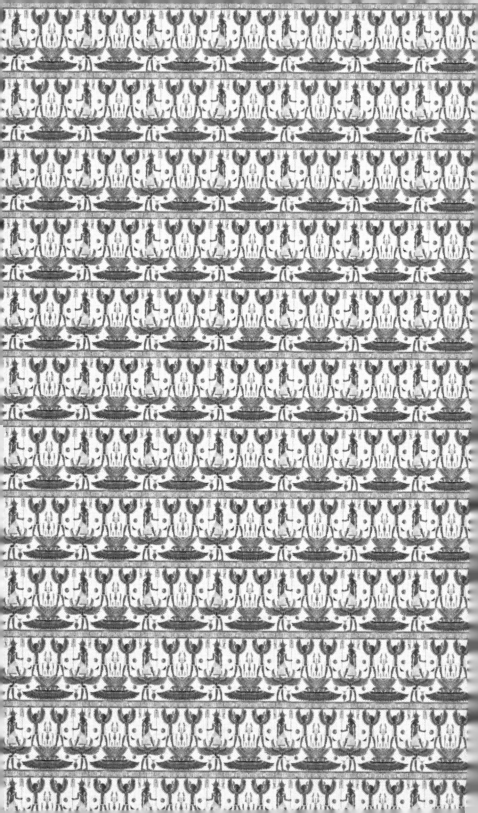

XLI: INFLUENCE OF EGYPTIAN RITUALS ON LATER CULTURES AND RELIGIONS

The influence of Egyptian rituals on later cultures and religions is a confirmation of the lasting heritage of ancient Egypt's religious and philosophical thought. As one of the cradles of civilization, Egypt's religious practices, opulent mythologies, and profound symbolism have permeated various cultures and religious traditions, leaving an undeniable mark on the spiritual territory of the ancient and modern worlds. This influence can be traced through the Hellenistic period, into the development of early Christian and Islamic practices, and even into contemporary New Age spiritual movements, demonstrating the eternal appeal and adaptability of Egyptian religious concepts. During the Hellenistic period, following Alexander the Great's conquest of Egypt, Greek and Egyptian religious practices began to intermingle, leading to the formation of syncretic deities and the adoption of Egyptian rituals within Greek practices. The cult of Isis, in particular, became all over throughout the Hellenistic world, extending as far as Rome. Isis was venerated as a universal goddess, embodying attributes of Greek, Roman, and other deities, and her worship incorporated Egyptian rituals, including processions, the use of sacred objects, and initiation rites. The mysteries of Isis, which promised personal salvation and eternal life to initiates, bore similarities to Egyptian funerary beliefs and can be seen as precursors to Christian notions of resurrection and redemption.

The influence of Egyptian rituals on early Christianity is evident in several practices and theological concepts. Early Christian communities in Egypt, known as Copts, integrated aspects of Egyptian religious symbolism into Christian iconography and liturgy. The use of the ankh, the ancient Egyptian symbol of life, was adapted by Coptic Christians as a representation of eternal life through Christ. Additionally, the Christian practice of monasticism has its roots in the ascetic traditions of ancient Egyptian religious life, where individuals would retreat into the desert to live a life of prayer and contemplation, seeking direct communion with the divine.

The veneration of saints and martyrs in Christianity, accompanied by the use of relics and the belief in their intercessory power, echoes the ancient Egyptian practice of venerating the deceased and seeking their intervention with the gods. The architectural layout and orientation of early Christian churches also show influences from Egyptian temple design, emphasizing the eastward direction of worship and the symbolic adventure from the earthly world to the divine.

In Islam, which also emerged within a cultural territory shaped by millennia of Egyptian religious thought, there are echoes of Egyptian ritual practices. The Islamic tradition of reciting prayers at specific times of the day parallels the ancient Egyptian practice of offering prayers and incantations to the sun god Ra at dawn, noon, and sunset. The Islamic emphasis on cleanliness and purification before prayer reflects ancient Egyptian purification rituals, which were essential for maintaining personal holiness and for the proper conduct of religious ceremonies.

In contemporary times, the fascination with ancient Egypt has led to the revival and reinterpretation of Egyptian rituals and symbolism within New Age and esoteric spiritual movements. Practices like meditation, the use of amulets for protection and healing, and the celebration of solstices and equinoxes draw encouragement from ancient Egyptian religious traditions. These modern adaptations often emphasize personal spiritual growth, healing, and the pursuit of mystical knowledge, themes that were central to Egyptian religious life.

The influence of Egyptian rituals on later cultures and religions underscores the profound effect of ancient Egypt's spiritual heritage on the development of religious thought and practice. Through the centuries, Egyptian rituals have been adapted, reinterpreted, and integrated into diverse religious traditions, reflecting both the universality of Egypt's religious concepts and the lasting human quest for understanding the divine. These influences highlight the enmeshment of humanity's spiritual history and the ongoing relevance of ancient wisdom in seeking to address the fundamental questions of existence, the afterlife, and the nature of the divine.

XLII: THE SIGNIFICANCE OF GOLD IN EGYPTIAN SYMBOLISM

The significance of gold in ancient Egyptian symbolism is deeply grounded in the civilization's religious beliefs, cosmology, and understanding of the divine. Gold, with its lasting luster and incorruptibility, was not merely valued for its aesthetic appeal or as a material of economic wealth but was imbued with profound symbolic meanings. It was associated with the sun, divinity, and eternal life, playing a central place in ritual practices, funerary rites, and the adornment of deities, pharaohs, and the elite. The use and reverence of gold in ancient Egyptian culture reflect its place as a material manifestation of the sacred, embodying the eternal aspects of the cosmos and the gods.

Gold's association with the sun god Ra was one of its most significant symbolic connections. The metal's radiant color and lasting nature were seen as reflective of the sun's eternal light and its unceasing cycle across the sky. Gold was respected as the flesh of the gods, particularly of Ra, who was believed to have golden skin. This belief was manifested in the creation of divine statues and religious artifacts, which were often crafted from gold to symbolize the gods' divine essence and immortality. The use of gold in religious contexts served to invoke the presence of the divine, drawing the gods closer to the earthly world and facilitating communion with them. In the context of pharaonic regalia and royal adornment, gold symbolized the pharaoh's divine nature and his place as the earthly embodiment of the gods. The pharaoh was often depicted wearing gold crowns, jewelry, and other accoutrements, signifying his divine right to rule, his association with the sun god, and his status as a living god among his people. Gold was integral to the regalia used in coronation ceremonies and other ritual practices, reinforcing the pharaoh's position as the mediator between the divine and mortal worlds and his responsibility to uphold Ma'at, the universal order.

Funerary practices and beliefs about the afterlife further underscore the symbolic significance of gold in ancient Egyptian culture. Gold was used extensively in the preparation of the dead for their adventure to the afterlife, all the way from the masks placed over the faces of mummies, like the famous mask of Tutankhamun, to the amulets and jewelry included in the burial assemblage. These gold items were believed to protect the deceased, ensuring their safe passage through the underworld and their rebirth into the afterlife. Gold's incorruptibility made it the perfect material to symbolize the deceased's hoped-for eternal existence, free from decay and the passage of time.

The use of gold in the construction and decoration of temples and tombs further illustrates its symbolic importance. Temples, as the dwelling places of the gods on earth, were adorned with gold to honor the deities and to create a fitting environment for worship and ritual practices. Tombs, particularly those of pharaohs and high officials, featured gold in their design and decoration, reflecting the belief in the deceased's divine transformation and their new existence among the gods.

The significance of gold in ancient Egyptian symbolism is multifaceted, reflecting the civilization's religious beliefs, ritual practices, and cosmological views. Gold was more than a material of physical value; it was a symbol of the divine, the eternal, and the transcendent aspects of existence. Through its use in religious artifacts, royal regalia, and funerary rites, gold served as a tangible expression of the ancient Egyptians' quest for immortality, their reverence for the gods, and their understanding of the universal order. The symbolism of gold in ancient Egyptian culture highlights the civilization's spiritual depth, its concern with life beyond death, and its pursuit of an eternal existence in harmony with the divine.

XLIII: THE RITUAL OF THE OPENING OF THE MOUTH CEREMONY

The Opening of the Mouth ceremony was a necessary ritual in ancient Egyptian religious practices, deeply embedded in their funerary traditions and beliefs about the afterlife. This ancient ritual, which dates back to the Old Kingdom, was performed to reanimate the mummy or a statue of the deceased, enabling the deceased to breathe, eat, see, hear, and speak in the afterlife, thereby ensuring their wellness and survival in the world of the dead. The ceremony symbolized the restoration of life's essential functions to the mummified body or statue, reflecting the Egyptians' belief in the possibility of life after death and the importance of maintaining a continuum between the mortal world and the eternal hereafter.

Originating from the mythological reanimation of Osiris by Isis and Nephthys, the ritual was integral to the process of mummification and burial, serving as the climax of the funerary rites. According to myth, after Osiris was murdered and dismembered by Seth, his body parts were scattered across Egypt. Isis, his sister-wife, along with Nephthys, gathered his remains and performed rites that restored life to Osiris, allowing him to become the ruler of the afterlife. This mythological backdrop provided the template for the Opening of the Mouth ceremony, linking the deceased with Osiris and ensuring their resurrection and continuation in the afterlife.

The ceremony was conducted by a priest, often the deceased's eldest son or another close male relative, who assumed the place of the funerary deity (usually Anubis or Horus) responsible for the ritual.

The priest, adorned in specific ceremonial attire, used an adze, a special ritualistic tool shaped like a lion's head and made from precious materials, to touch the mummy or statue's mouth, eyes, ears, and nostrils. This act was accompanied by recitations of spells and incantations, drawn from funerary texts like the Pyramid Texts, Coffin Texts, and the Book of the Dead, intended to restore the deceased's senses and living functions. The ritual encompassed several stages, each aimed at reanimating different aspects of the deceased's being. It began with purification rites involving the sprinkling of water and the burning of incense to cleanse the sacred space and the participants. Offerings of food, drink, and clothing were made to the deceased, symbolizing the provision of sustenance and protection in the afterlife. Following the physical touching of the mummy or statue's sensory and speech organs with the adze, further rites were performed to protect the deceased from evil forces and to reaffirm their identity and status in the afterlife.

The Opening of the Mouth ceremony was not confined to the funerary context but was also performed on statues of deities and the deceased in temples and tombs. This extended use of the ritual underscored the belief in the animate nature of statues, which were respected as alternative dwellings for the ka (spirit) of the gods or the deceased. By performing the ritual on statues, the Egyptians ensured that the divine or mortal essence residing within them was revitalized, maintaining the efficacy of the statues as recipients of worship and interaction with the divine.

The Opening of the Mouth ceremony was a complex and multifaceted ritual that encapsulated the ancient Egyptians' beliefs about death, the afterlife, and the possibility of eternal life. Through this ritual, the deceased were equipped with the means to live again, to interact with the gods and the living, and to partake in the offerings made to them. The ceremony reflects the Egyptians' profound understanding of the afterlife as an extension of mortal existence, where the dead required the same physical and spiritual faculties as the living to ensure their wellness and happiness. Through the ritual practices associated with the Opening of the Mouth, the ancient Egyptians sought to bridge the gap between the world of the living and the dead, securing a place for the deceased in the eternal world and affirming the continuity of life beyond the grave.

XLIV: ⴕHE CONCEPT OF dUAⴕ: ⴕHE EGYPⴕIAN UNDERWORLD

The concept of Duat, the Egyptian underworld, is a central element in the ancient Egyptian understanding of the afterlife, cosmology, and the continuation of existence beyond death. This complex and multifaceted world was not merely a place of darkness and oblivion but a parallel world where the deceased began on a perilous adventure towards rebirth and immortality. The Duat was both a physical space, believed to lie beneath the earth, and a spiritual dimension, intercharted with the cycles of the sun and the universal order. Its depiction in ancient Egyptian religious texts, funerary inscriptions, and tomb paintings reveals an opulent atlas of beliefs, rituals, and symbolism, reflecting the Egyptians' profound engagement with the mysteries of life, death, and the afterlife. Central to the concept of the Duat was the adventure of the sun god Ra through the underworld during the night. Each evening, Ra descended into the Duat, sailing in his barque through its twelve regions, corresponding to the twelve hours of the night. This adventure was fraught with dangers, as Ra and his entourage faced challenges and adversaries, including the serpent Apophis, the embodiment of chaos and destruction. The successful navigation of the Duat and the defeat of Apophis were essential for the rebirth of Ra at dawn, symbolizing the triumph of order over chaos, light over darkness, and the renewal of life. This daily cycle was a powerful metaphor for the deceased's adventure through the underworld, promising the possibility of rebirth and the continuation of existence in the afterlife.

The Book of the Dead, the Book of Gates, and the Amduat are among the key texts that provide insight into the Egyptian concept of the Duat and the adventure of the deceased. These texts, often inscribed on tomb walls, sarcophagi, and funerary papyri, served as guides for the deceased, offering spells, prayers, and incantations to aid in their passage through the underworld. The detailed descriptions of the Duat in these texts uncover a world of giant landscapes, divine inhabitants, and complex rituals, underscoring the Egyptians' belief in the afterlife as an active and dynamic existence.

The deceased's adventure through the Duat was envisaged as a process of purification, judgment, and transformation. Upon entering the underworld, the deceased faced a series of trials, including the weighing of the heart against the feather of Ma'at, the goddess of truth and universal order. This judgment determined the deceased's worthiness to proceed towards immortality. A heart weighed down by sin was devoured by Ammit, the devourer of the dead, resulting in the annihilation of the individual's existence. Those who passed the judgment were granted access to the Field of Reeds, a paradisiacal world where they could live in peace and contentment, enjoying an idealized version of their earthly life.

The place of funerary rituals, amulets, and spells was necessary in assisting the deceased in their adventure through the Duat. The Opening of the Mouth ceremony, the provision of funerary offerings, and the inclusion of the Book of the Dead among the grave goods were all aimed at equipping the deceased with the knowledge and protection needed to navigate the underworld successfully. These practices reflect the ancient Egyptians' active engagement with the afterlife, where the wellness of the deceased in the Duat was ensured through the actions of the living.

The concept of the Duat in ancient Egyptian religion includes the civilization's nuanced understanding of death and the afterlife. It was a world of both danger and potential, where the deceased underwent a transformative adventure, reflecting the cycles of nature and the universal order. Through their beliefs, rituals, and funerary practices, the ancient Egyptians sought to navigate the mysteries of the Duat, securing a place of eternal existence for the deceased among the stars, in the presence of the gods. The Duat, with its complex geography, divine inhabitants, and moral challenges, remains a powerful symbol of the ancient Egyptian quest for immortality, highlighting the civilization's profound reflections on the nature of existence, the afterlife, and the human desire for continuity beyond death.

XLV: Egyptian Temple Rituals and Daily Offerings

Egyptian temple rituals and daily offerings constituted a core aspect of ancient Egyptian religious practice, reflecting the civilization's profound devotion to the gods and the central place of the temple as a bridge between the divine and the mortal worlds. These rituals were carefully structured and performed with the utmost reverence, aimed at sustaining the gods, maintaining universal order, and ensuring the wellness of both the state and its people. Through daily offerings, ceremonial rites, and the recitation of prayers and hymns, the priests of ancient Egypt sought to appease the gods, secure their favor, and avert chaos from the land. The temple itself was viewed not merely as a place of worship but as the actual dwelling place of the deity. As such, temples were designed to reflect the cosmos's order, with architecture and layout symbolizing the creation of the universe. The most sacred area of the temple, the sanctuary, housed the cult statue, a physical representation of the god to whom the temple was dedicated. This statue was believed to be imbued with the deity's living essence, and it was to this effigy that the daily rituals were primarily directed.

The core of daily temple ritual was the offering ceremony, conducted three times a day —morning, midday, and evening. This ceremony was performed by priests who had undergone rigorous purification rituals to ensure their worthiness to stand in the presence of the divine.

The first act of the morning ritual involved the "Opening of the Mouth" of the sanctuary's doors, followed by the "Opening of the Mouth" and eyes of the deity's statue, symbolically awakening the god. The priests would then proceed to cleanse the statue with sacred water, dress it in fresh garments, and adorn it with jewelry, effectively renewing the god's physical form.

Following the purification and adornment, offerings of food, drink, and incense were presented to the deity. These offerings were believed to sustain the god, allowing them to continue their divine functions of creation and maintenance of the universal order. The food offerings typically included bread, beer, meat, fruits, and other delicacies, while libations of water and milk were poured out before the statue. Incense, with its fragrant smoke, was burned not just for its pleasing aroma but also for its purifying qualities, symbolizing the transformation of the offerings into spiritual sustenance for the god.

The recitation of prayers and hymns accompanied the physical offerings, invoking the deity's attributes and recounting their mythological deeds. These texts often appealed to the god's benevolence, requesting protection, health, and prosperity for the pharaoh, the temple, and the people. The prayers also reaffirmed the reciprocal relationship between the gods and their worshippers, wherein human devotion and offerings were exchanged for divine favor and assistance. After the morning offerings, the temple was closed to the public, and only priests were permitted to enter the inner sanctuaries. However, the outer courtyards of the temple remained open for individuals to bring their own offerings and petitions to the gods. These personal devotions complemented the official rituals, reflecting the integral place of the temple in the spiritual life of the community.

The significance of temple rituals and daily offerings extended beyond the immediate acts of worship, embodying the ancient Egyptians' worldview. The rituals were seen as essential to the maintenance of Ma'at, the principle of universal order, balance, and justice. By sustaining the gods through offerings and rituals, the Egyptians believed they were ensuring the continued functioning of the cosmos according to divine law. The prosperity of the land, the annual flooding of the Nile, and the success of the pharaoh's reign were all seen as dependent on the proper performance of these rites.

Egyptian temple rituals and daily offerings were a complex relationship of religious devotion, cosmology, and social order. Through these practices, the ancient Egyptians sought to secure the favor of the gods, maintain the balance of the universe, and ensure the wellness of their civilization. The rituals mirrored a profound understanding of the reciprocal relationship between the divine and the mortal, where human actions in the temple mirrored universal processes and divine will. This intricate system of worship underscores the centrality of religion in ancient Egyptian society and its lasting heritage in understanding the divine.

XLVI: EGYPTIAN GODS AND THE PHARAOH'S POWER

The connection between the Egyptian gods and the pharaoh's power is a fundamental aspect of ancient Egyptian religion and governance, illustrating the intricate charting of theology and monarchy that defined the civilization. This relationship was grounded in the belief that the pharaoh was not merely a king but a divine or semi-divine figure, embodying the gods' presence on Earth and acting as their chief intermediary. The pharaoh's power and legitimacy were thus seen as directly derived from the gods, and his rule was respected as a reflection of the universal order, or Ma'at, which he was charged to uphold. This divine kingship was central to Egyptian identity, influencing every aspect of society from architecture to daily religious practices. The pharaoh was often identified with Horus, the falcon god of kingship and the sky, all the way from the earliest periods of Egyptian history. As the son of Osiris and Isis, Horus represented the living king on Earth, while Osiris symbolized the pharaoh in the afterlife. This identification with Horus established the pharaoh as the legitimate ruler, sanctioned by divine heritage and bound to the cycle of universal regeneration. The Eye of Horus, a symbol of protection, royal power, and good health, became an emblem of the pharaoh's divine right to rule, signifying the god's watchful presence over the king and his domain.

Additionally, the pharaoh was respected as the "son of Ra," the sun god, further emphasizing his divine affiliation and the celestial source of his authority. Ra was the principal deity of the Egyptian pantheon, associated with creation, the order of the universe, and the cycle of life and death. By associating themselves with Ra, pharaohs underscored their place as the upholders of universal order and the protectors of their people. The solar disk, often depicted above the pharaoh's name, symbolized this divine connection, reinforcing the idea that the king's power was illuminated and energized by the sun itself.

The pharaoh's relationship with other deities also underscored his multifaceted place as ruler, warrior, and religious leader. For example, his association with Amun, a creator god who rose to prominence during the New Kingdom, highlighted the pharaoh's place in maintaining religious and social harmony. The amalgamation of Amun and Ra into Amun-Ra during this period further solidified the pharaoh's status as a divine intermediary, responsible for the prosperity and stability of the kingdom through his connection to this supreme deity. The ritual and ceremonial duties of the pharaoh served to reinforce his divine status and his relationship with the gods. He was responsible for performing key religious ceremonies, dedicating temples, and making offerings to the gods, acting as the primary conduit through which the gods communicated their will and blessings to the people. These acts were not just religious formalities but essential to the sustenance of the gods and the universal order they embodied. The pharaoh's participation in these rituals was a public demonstration of his divine right and duty to rule, as well as a reaffirmation of the gods' favor and support for his reign.

In the world of funerary practices, the connection between the pharaoh and the gods was most explicitly articulated. Tombs and mortuary temples were constructed to ensure the king's divine transformation and ascension to the afterlife, where he would join the gods and continue to protect Egypt. The Pyramid Texts, Coffin Texts, and the Book of the Dead contain spells and incantations that were designed to guide the deceased pharaoh through the dangers of the underworld, secure his identification with Osiris, and ensure his resurrection and immortality among the gods. These texts underscore the belief in the pharaoh's divine essence and his eternal place as the guardian of Egypt's welfare.

The connection between the Egyptian gods and the pharaoh's power is thus a reflection of the civilization's deeply religious worldview, where the divine order was manifested through the monarchy, and the king was both a god on Earth and the servant of the gods. This relationship was central to the functioning of Egyptian society, ensuring the alignment of earthly rule with universal principles and securing the kingdom's prosperity and stability through divine favor. The pharaoh's divine kingship was a complex relationship of theology, ritual, and governance, embodying the ancient Egyptians' quest to harmonize human existence with the eternal order of the universe.

XLVII: THE PLACE OF SACRED ANIMALS IN EGYPTIAN RELIGIOUS PRACTICES

The place of sacred animals in ancient Egyptian religious practices is a profound reflection of the civilization's complex belief system, which intertwined the natural world with the divine. In Egypt, animals were not merely respected as gods in their own right but were also respected as manifestations of deities, symbols of divine attributes, and essential participants in religious rituals. This reverence for sacred animals is evident across a wide spectrum of Egyptian religious life, from temple worship and funerary rites to daily practices and state ceremonies.

Central to the Egyptian understanding of sacred animals was the concept of the "ba," a term that denotes an aspect of the soul or a divine manifestation. Many gods were associated with specific animals respected as to be their "ba" or earthly embodiment. For example, the god Horus was often depicted as a falcon or with a falcon's head, embodying the sky and kingship's divine attributes. Similarly, the goddess Bastet was associated with the domestic cat, symbolizing fertility, motherhood, and the protective qualities of the sun's warmth. These associations were not arbitrary but stemmed from the Egyptians' keen observation of animal behavior and characteristics, which they saw as reflections of the gods' powers and roles within the cosmos.

The practice of keeping sacred animals in temples was all over in ancient Egypt. Temples dedicated to particular deities often housed animals respected as living incarnations of those gods. These animals were treated with great reverence, provided with luxurious accommodations, and cared for by a dedicated priesthood. The Apis bull, associated with the god Ptah and later with Osiris, is one of the most well-known examples of a sacred temple animal. The selection of the Apis bull followed specific criteria, and its life and death were marked by elaborate rituals reflecting its sacred status. Upon death, the Apis bull was mummified and buried with honors in the Serapeum at Saqqara, underscoring its significance in the religious and ceremonial life of Egypt.

Sacred animals also held a necessary place in divination and oracles. The behavior of certain animals was observed and interpreted as messages from the gods. For instance, the movement of the Apis bull was closely watched for omens, and its actions were respected as divine responses to questions posed by the faithful or the state. This practice of using animals as oracles demonstrates the deep integration of sacred animals into the mechanisms of religious consultation and decision-making. In funerary practices, sacred animals were believed to provide protection and guidance for the deceased in the afterlife. Amulets in the shapes of sacred animals were commonly placed among the mummy's wrappings, serving as magical wards against evil and as symbols of divine protection. The jackal, associated with Anubis, the god of mummification and the afterlife, was a particularly potent symbol, embodying the protective and guiding roles required for the deceased's adventure through the underworld.

The reverence for sacred animals extended beyond temple and funerary contexts, permeating daily life in ancient Egypt. Animals were featured prominently in Egyptian art and literature, not just as divine symbols but also as integral parts of the natural order, which was itself imbued with sacred significance. The respectful treatment of animals, including practices like the provision of food and water for stray dogs and cats, mirrored a broader ethos of respect for life that was grounded in religious belief. The place of sacred animals in Egyptian religious practices thus reflects the civilization's intricate and holistic worldview, which saw the divine in every aspect of the natural world. Sacred animals were not merely symbols or representations of the gods but were respected as active participants in the religious life of Egypt, serving as intermediaries between the divine and human worlds, embodying the gods' presence on Earth, and participating in the maintenance of universal order. Through the veneration of sacred animals, the ancient Egyptians expressed their understanding of the enmeshment of all life, the omnipresence of the divine, and the profound respect for the natural world that characterized their religious and philosophical outlook.

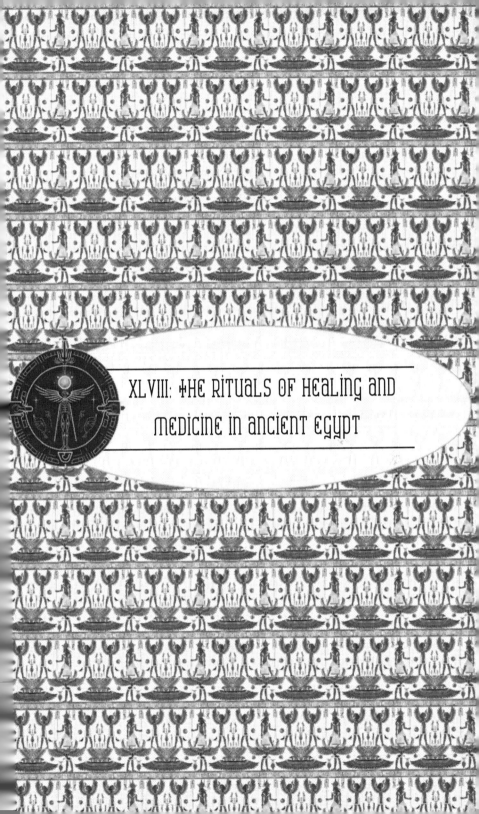

XLVIII: THE RITUALS OF HEALING AND MEDICINE IN ANCIENT EGYPT

The rituals of healing and medicine in ancient Egypt were deeply intercharted with the civilization's religious beliefs and practices, reflecting an understanding of health and illness that integrated the physical, spiritual, and magical worlds. The ancient Egyptians did not draw a sharp distinction between medical treatment and religious or magical practices; instead, they saw these approaches as complementary, each playing a necessary place in the restoration of health. This holistic view of medicine is evident in the surviving medical papyri, temple inscriptions, and artifacts, which uncover a sophisticated approach to healing that combined empirical knowledge with ritual and incantation.

Central to the Egyptian concept of health was the idea of Ma'at, the universal principle of order, balance, and harmony. Illness and disease were perceived as manifestations of disorder, either physical or spiritual, resulting from an imbalance within the body or from malevolent forces. Healing rituals, therefore, aimed not just to treat the physical symptoms but also to restore the patient's spiritual and universal balance, invoking the protection of the gods and employing magical spells to repel harmful entities. Priests and physicians, often one and the same, held a key place in the administration of healing rituals. These individuals were highly trained in both the medical arts and religious rites, equipped with knowledge passed down through generations. The House of Life, an institution attached to major temples, served as a center for learning and healing, where medical texts were studied and copied, and where treatments were administered. Priests-physicians would diagnose ailments, prescribe treatments, and perform healing rituals, invoking specific deities associated with health and medicine, like Sekhmet, the lioness goddess of war and healing, or Thoth, the ibis-headed god of wisdom and scribe of the gods, who was also credited with medical knowledge. Healing rituals often involved the recitation of spells and incantations, designed to address the spiritual or magical aspects of the ailment. These spells, which were believed to harness the power of the spoken word, were recited over the patient or inscribed on amulets, papyri, or the walls of temples and tombs. The Ebers Papyrus and the Edwin Smith Papyrus, among others, contain examples of such spells, alongside empirical treatments and surgical procedures, illustrating the integration of magical and medical practices. The use of amulets was another common feature of Egyptian healing rituals. These objects, often inscribed with spells or images of deities, were worn by the patient to ward off evil spirits and to attract divine protection. Amulets in the shape of specific body parts, animals, or symbols were used to target particular ailments, drawing on the magical properties associated with these forms to effect healing.

Offerings and sacrifices to the gods were also integral to the healing process, serving to appease the deities and to solicit their intervention on behalf of the patient. Temples dedicated to healing deities, like the temple of Sekhmet at Karnak, were sites of pilgrimage for those seeking cures for their ailments. Here, patients would participate in rituals, offer votive gifts, and sometimes spend the night within the temple precincts, hoping to receive visions or dreams that would uncover the path to healing.

The practice of incubation, or temple sleep, was a significant ritual in Egyptian medicine. Patients would sleep within the sacred space of a temple, believing that the god would visit them in their dreams to offer diagnosis, prognosis, or treatment. This practice underscores the Egyptians' belief in the gods' direct involvement in the healing process and their reliance on divine revelation as a means of addressing health concerns.

The rituals of healing and medicine in ancient Egypt reflect the civilization's holistic approach to health, which encompassed the physical, spiritual, and universal dimensions of humanity's existence. Through a combination of empirical knowledge, ritual practice, and magical incantation, the ancient Egyptians sought to restore balance and harmony, invoking the gods' power to heal and protect. These practices uncover a sophisticated understanding of the relationship between body, spirit, and the divine, and highlight the integral place of religion and magic in the maintenance of health and the treatment of disease in ancient Egyptian society.

XLIX: THE SYMBOLISM OF THE EYE OF HORUS AND THE EYE OF RA

The symbolism of the Eye of Horus and the Eye of Ra occupies a central place in ancient Egyptian religious beliefs, practices, and iconography, reflecting complex layers of mythology, cosmology, and philosophical thought. These two symbols, while often used interchangeably in modern interpretations, held distinct meanings and associations for the ancient Egyptians, each grounded in different mythological traditions and embodying unique aspects of divine power, protection, and healing.

The Eye of Horus

The Eye of Horus, also known as "Wedjat," is a powerful symbol of protection, health, and restoration. Its origins lie in the myth of Horus, the falcon-headed god of the sky, kingship, and victory, and his epic battle with Seth, the god of chaos and disorder. During their conflict, Horus's left eye was damaged or torn out, only to be restored or "made whole" again by Thoth, the god of wisdom, magic, and healing. This narrative of loss and restoration made the Eye of Horus a potent symbol of healing, wholeness, and the triumph of order over chaos.

In ancient Egyptian religious thought, the Eye of Horus was more than a mythological motif; it was an amulet of great protective power, used extensively in funerary practices and magical rites. The eye was often depicted as a highly stylized eye and eyebrow, with the characteristic 'teardrop' marking beneath it, representing the markings of a falcon. As an amulet, it were to ward off evil, ensure the safety and health of the bearer, and provide the deceased with the ability to see, eat, and interact with the living world, thus facilitating their adventure through the afterlife.

The Eye of Horus also held numerical significance, with its various parts symbolizing the six senses, including thought, in addition to the traditional five senses. Each part was associated with a fraction, together summing to one, symbolizing wholeness and the integration of the senses in achieving complete perception.

The Eye of Ra

The Eye of Ra, by contrast, embodies the solar and fiery aspects of the sun god Ra's power. It is often represented by a fierce lioness or a cobra wearing the solar disk, symbolizing its place as the protector of Ra and the enforcer of his will. The Eye of Ra was respected as an extension of Ra's power, acting independently to subdue his enemies and as a guardian against the forces of chaos. Mythologically, the Eye of Ra is associated with the goddesses Hathor, Sekhmet, and Bastet, among others, who could manifest as the vengeful aspect of Ra's power. One myth recounts how the Eye of Ra, in the form of the lioness goddess Sekhmet, was unleashed upon humanity as punishment for rebellion. Her rampage was halted only when she was tricked into drinking beer dyed red to resemble blood, becoming so intoxicated that she ceased her slaughter. This myth underscores the dual nature of the Eye of Ra as both a source of destruction and a protector against external threats to universal order.

Symbolic Relationship and Integration

While distinct, the symbols of the Eye of Horus and the Eye of Ra were often merged or used complementarily in Egyptian symbolism, reflecting the fluid nature of Egyptian religious iconography and the overlapping roles of deities. Both eyes were invoked for protection, healing, and the maintenance of Ma'at, the universal order, representing the vigilant gaze of the divine over the mortal world. In funerary texts and amulets, the Eyes could stand for the sun and moon, embodying the universal and eternal presence of the divine in the daily cycle of life, death, and rebirth. They were also symbols of royal power and legitimacy, signifying the pharaoh's place as the earthly embodiment of divine order and his capacity to unite the two lands of Upper and Lower Egypt.

In essence, the symbolism of the Eye of Horus and the Eye of Ra includes the ancient Egyptians' complex religious and cosmological beliefs. These symbols served as reminders of the gods' protective powers, the possibility of healing and restoration, and the ever-present tension between order and chaos. Through the veneration of the Eyes, the ancient Egyptians sought the gods' favor, protection from harm, and the assurance of Ma'at in their lives and in the afterlife, illustrating the profound spiritual and philosophical depth of their civilization.

L: The Rituals and Symbolism of Egyptian Royal Births

The rituals and symbolism of Egyptian royal births were deeply embedded within the cultural and religious map of ancient Egyptian society, reflecting the civilization's complex beliefs about divinity, kingship, and the cosmos. Royal births were not merely familial events but state affairs, enveloped in rituals and symbols that underscored the divine nature of the monarchy and its necessary place in maintaining the universal order, or Ma'at. These events were carefully orchestrated to emphasize the pharaoh's divine lineage, the continuity of divine favor upon the royal family, and the future ruler's destined place as the intermediary between the gods and the people.

Divine Conception and Birth

The mythology surrounding royal births often included the theme of divine conception. According to these myths, the reigning pharaoh was sired by a god, most commonly Amun, who visited the queen in the guise of her husband or through a divine epiphany. This divine paternity underscored the god-like status of the pharaoh and legitimized the royal offspring's right to the throne. The story of the divine birth of Hatshepsut, as depicted in her mortuary temple at Deir el-Bahri, acts as a prime example, illustrating the god Amun's place in her conception, thereby reinforcing her legitimacy and divine right to rule.

Rituals and Ceremonies

The actual birth of a royal child was accompanied by a series of rituals designed to protect the mother and child, ensure a successful delivery, and welcome the newborn into the world with divine blessings. These rituals often invoked the protection of specific deities associated with childbirth and motherhood, like Taweret, Bes, and Hathor. The presence of these deities in birthing amulets, spells, and the decoration of birthing chambers highlighted their intercessory roles in safeguarding the royal birth process. Following the birth, naming ceremonies were conducted to imbue the royal offspring with their identities and destinies. Names were of profound significance in ancient Egyptian culture, believed to contain power and influence over the bearer's life. Royal children were often given several names, each reflecting aspects of their hoped-for character, divine protection, and anticipated reign. These naming ceremonies were imbued with rituals that called upon the gods to bless and protect the child, ensuring their successful future as Egypt's ruler.

Symbolism in Royal Birth Imagery

The symbolism in the imagery associated with royal births further illustrated the event's universal significance. Temples and monuments often featured reliefs depicting the divine conception and birth of the pharaoh, surrounded by gods and goddesses, emphasizing the royal child's divine origins and the gods' active interest in the welfare of Egypt. The iconography used in these depictions was opulent in symbols of fertility, divine protection, and royal authority, like lotus flowers, solar disks, and the ankh, symbolizing life.

Integration with Universal Order

The rituals and symbolism surrounding royal births were also deeply connected to the Egyptians' understanding of the cosmos and the natural order. The cyclical flooding of the Nile, which brought fertility to the land, was often paralleled with the fertility of the queen and the birth of the royal heir, symbolizing the renewal of life and the continuation of divine blessings upon the land. This connection reinforced the idea that the monarchy was integral to the maintenance of Ma'at, with the birth of a royal child heralding the perpetuation of universal harmony and balance.

Heritage and Continuity

The importance placed on royal births extended beyond the immediate celebration to underscore the lasting heritage and continuity of the divine monarchy. Royal children were educated and groomed for their future roles from an early age, with their births heralding the continuation of the dynastic line and the lasting relationship between the gods and the royal family. This preparation often included religious and administrative training, ensuring that the future pharaoh would be well-equipped to uphold his divine duties and maintain Ma'at. The rituals and symbolism of Egyptian royal births were not merely celebratory acknowledgments of a new life but profound expressions of the civilization's religious beliefs, political ideology, and cosmological understanding. Through these practices, ancient Egyptians articulated their convictions about divine kingship, the sacred nature of the royal lineage, and the integral place of the monarchy in the universal order. The birth of a royal child was a moment of both temporal joy and eternal significance, marking the continuation of divine favor upon Egypt and the renewal of the covenant between the gods, the land, and its people.

LI: THE RELIGIOUS SIGNIFICANCE OF EGYPTIAN PYRAMIDS

The Egyptian pyramids, monumental tombs erected for the country's pharaohs, are among the most lasting symbols of ancient Egypt's architectural, cultural, and religious achievements. Far from being mere burial places, these structures hold profound religious significance, encapsulating the civilization's beliefs about death, the afterlife, and the cosmos. Their construction during the Old and Middle Kingdoms, especially the Fourth Dynasty's great pyramids at Giza, reflects a complex relationship of religious symbolism, royal power, and cosmological thought.

Universal Symbolism and Alignment

The pyramids were designed as universal symbols, embodying the Egyptians' view of the universe and the afterlife. Their shape, mirroring the Benben stone or the primeval mound that emerged from the waters of chaos at the beginning of time, represented the creation of the world. This connection to the creation myth imbued the pyramids with the power of rebirth and regeneration, offering the deceased pharaoh a direct link to the cosmos and ensuring his resurrection among the gods. The precise alignment of the pyramids with the stars further underscores their religious significance. The sides of the Great Pyramid of Giza, for instance, are closely aligned with the four cardinal points, reflecting the Egyptians' advanced understanding of astronomy and its religious implications. This alignment was likely intended to facilitate the soul's adventure to the afterlife, with the northern alignment pointing towards the imperishable stars, where the deceased ruler would join the circumpolar stars that never set, symbolizing eternity and indestructibility.

The Pyramids as a Part of a Larger Religious Complex

Each pyramid was part of a larger funerary complex that included temples, causeways, and smaller satellite pyramids, reflecting a comprehensive vision of the afterlife. The valley temple, connected to the pyramid temple by a long causeway, served as the site for the initial stages of the funeral rites and the mummification process. These temples were not just spaces for worship and offerings but also served as symbolic passageways for the pharaoh's soul from the earthly world to the divine. The inclusion of subsidiary pyramids for queens and courtiers further focuses on the belief in a stratified afterlife, where proximity to the pharaoh ensured a favorable position in the next world.

The Pyramid Texts

The religious significance of the pyramids is perhaps most explicitly articulated in the Pyramid Texts, first appearing in the pyramid of

Unas at Saqqara. These inscriptions, comprising spells, hymns, and prayers, are among the oldest religious texts in the world. They were intended to protect the pharaoh's remains, repel malevolent forces, and provide the knowledge necessary for navigating the afterlife. The texts uncover a deep engagement with the mysteries of death and rebirth, offering insight into the Egyptians' beliefs about the soul's adventure to the afterlife, the importance of maintaining Ma'at, and the pharaoh's divine place in the universal order.

Theological Implications

The construction of the pyramids was a theological statement, affirming the pharaoh's god-like status and his necessary place in maintaining the balance between the earthly and divine worlds. The pharaoh was believed to become one with Osiris, god of the dead and ruler of the underworld, upon his death. The pyramid, as his tomb, served as the point of transition, where the king would begin on his adventure through the Duat (the underworld) to achieve resurrection and immortality. This belief system necessitated elaborate rituals and the creation of monumental architecture to secure the pharaoh's afterlife, reflecting the interdependence of religion, monarchy, and society in ancient Egypt.

In summary, the religious significance of Egyptian pyramids transcends their physical grandeur, embodying the ancient Egyptians' profound engagement with questions of life, death, and the cosmos. These structures were not mere tombs but symbols of the pharaoh's adventure to immortality, reflecting a civilization where architecture, religion, and politics were inextricably linked. The pyramids remain a confirmation of ancient Egypt's complex religious beliefs and its lasting fascination with the afterlife, offering modern observers a window into the spiritual life of one of history's most enigmatic civilizations.

LII: THE WORSHIP OF RA: SUN GOD AND CREATOR DEITY

The worship of Ra, the sun god and creator deity, stands at the heart of ancient Egyptian religion, encapsulating the civilization's profound reverence for the sun as the source of life, order, and universal harmony. Ra, also known as Re, was not just venerated as the god of the sun but also as the supreme creator, whose very utterance brought the universe into being. The cult of Ra, centered in Heliopolis, became one of the most influential and lasting aspects of Egyptian religious life, influencing theology, temple worship, and the daily lives of the ancient Egyptians.

Ra's Central Place in Egyptian Cosmology

In Egyptian cosmology, Ra's significance extended beyond his identity as the sun god. He was the embodiment of creation itself, with the rising sun symbolizing the rebirth of the world each morning. Ra's adventure across the sky in his solar barque, the "Mandjet," represented the cycle of life, death, and rebirth, with his passage through the underworld at night reflecting the struggle against chaos and darkness. This daily cycle was central to the Egyptian understanding of time, regeneration, and the afterlife, making Ra a necessary figure in the universal order.

The Mythology of Ra

Mythologically, Ra was said to have created himself from the primordial chaos, then created all forms of life through his thoughts and words. This act of self-creation and following creation of the world established Ra not just as a king among the gods but also as the progenitor of kingship, emphasizing the divine right of the pharaohs who were respected as his earthly embodiments. The mythology surrounding Ra is opulent and varied, including tales of his battle with the serpent Apophis, a symbol of chaos, which Ra defeated daily to ensure the continuation of the cosmos.

Worship and Rituals

The worship of Ra involved elaborate rituals and ceremonies conducted by priests in the temples dedicated to him. The most significant of these temples was the Great Sun Temple at Heliopolis, where rituals focused on the solar and creative aspects of Ra's nature. Daily rituals in these temples mirrored the adventure of the sun, with morning rituals welcoming Ra at dawn, midday rituals honoring his zenith, and evening rituals ensuring his safe passage into the underworld. Offerings of food, drink, and incense were made to Ra's statue, believed to house his presence, and hymns praising his glory and seeking his protection were sung by the temple choirs.

The Symbolism of Ra

Ra was often depicted as a man with the head of a falcon, crowned with a solar disk encircled by a cobra, symbolizing his dominion over the sky and his protective powers. The obelisk and the pyramid, both symbols of the sun's rays, were architectural embodiments of Ra's power, serving as tangible manifestations of his divine light and energy. The Eye of Ra, personified by the goddesses Hathor, Sekhmet, and Bastet, was a symbol of his protective and vengeful aspects, capable of both creating and destroying.

The Syncretism of Ra

The worship of Ra did not exist in isolation but was characterized by a remarkable degree of syncretism with other deities. The most notable of these was the amalgamation of Ra with Amun, a local Theban god, to form Amun-Ra, a composite deity who combined Amun's hidden aspects with Ra's visible power. This syncretism mirrored the fluid nature of Egyptian theology, where the attributes and functions of gods could merge in response to political and social changes, enhancing the deity's relevance and appeal.

The Heritage of Ra's Worship

The worship of Ra endured for millennia, adapting to the changing religious territory of Egypt. The sun god's cult influenced the development of solar theology, with following deities like Atum, Khepri, and Horakhty being incorporated into the solar pantheon, each representing different aspects of the sun's adventure and its life-giving power. The reverence for Ra also underscored the pharaoh's place as the "Son of Ra," reinforcing the king's divine mandate and his central place in maintaining Ma'at. So, the worship of Ra includes the ancient Egyptians' complex relationship with the divine, highlighting the sun's central place in their cosmology, religious practices, and understanding of kingship. Ra's lasting heritage is a confirmation of the sun god's integral place in Egyptian religion, symbolizing the unending cycle of life, the triumph over chaos, and the perpetuation of universal order. Through the worship of Ra, the ancient Egyptians expressed their deepest spiritual beliefs and their unstoppable faith in the sun's power to renew, protect, and sustain the world.

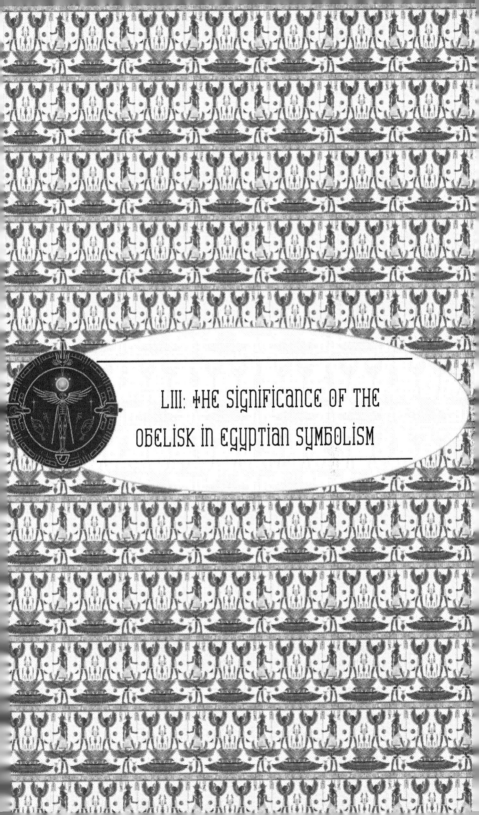

LIII: THE SIGNIFICANCE OF THE OBELISK IN EGYPTIAN SYMBOLISM

The obelisk, a quintessential emblem of ancient Egyptian civilization, stands as a confirmation of the Egyptians' architectural genius, religious fervor, and cosmological insights. These monumental stone pillars, tapering to a point at the top and often inscribed with hieroglyphs, were not merely decorative but deeply imbued with symbolic meanings and religious significance. Erected at the entrances of temples or in their courtyards, obelisks were dedicated to the sun god Ra, embodying the rays of the sun and serving as tangible manifestations of the deity's power, presence, and protection.

Architectural and Cosmological Symbolism

The architectural form of the obelisk, with its pyramidal peak, mirrors the benben, a primordial mound that, according to Egyptian creation myths, emerged from the chaotic waters at the beginning of time. This shape also echoes the pyramidal rays of the sun, reinforcing the obelisk's association with solar worship and the sun god Ra. The pointed tip, known as the pyramidion, was often covered in gold or electrum (a mixture of gold and silver), materials that, due to their lasting luster and incorruptibility, were associated with the eternal aspects of the divine. This reflective capstone captured the first and last light of the sun, symbolizing the daily rebirth of the sun and reinforcing the obelisk's place as a solar symbol.

Religious and Ritual Significance

Obelisks were religious monuments par excellence, serving as focal points for rituals and offerings to the sun god. Their placement at temple entrances or near altars was strategic, designed to sanctify the space and create a direct link between the earth and the divine world. The inscriptions on obelisks often included prayers, hymns to the sun god, and the names and titles of the pharaohs who commissioned them, serving both as religious texts and as assertions of the king's piety, divine favor, and legitimacy. The erection of an obelisk was a ritual in itself, involving ceremonies that consecrated the monument and invoked the presence of the deity. These rituals underscored the belief in the obelisk as a living embodiment of the god's power, capable of channeling divine energy and blessings to the temple, the king, and the land of Egypt. The obelisk's place in these ceremonies highlights its significance as a religious artifact, not merely a monument to human achievement or royal ambition.

Symbol of Ma'at

The obelisk also symbolized Ma'at, the principle of universal order, truth, and balance that was central to Egyptian religion and governance. By reaching from the earth to the heavens, the obelisk represented the pharaoh's place as the intermediary between the gods and the people, maintaining Ma'at through his actions and decrees. The stability (djed) and continuity (ankh) represented by the obelisk were necessary to the preservation of universal order, reflecting the ancient Egyptians' worldview where architecture, religion, and political authority were interlinked.

Historical and Cultural Heritage

The significance of the obelisk transcended the bounds of ancient Egypt, influencing later cultures and civilizations. In the Roman period, obelisks were transported to Rome to adorn circuses and public spaces, symbols of Egypt's subjugation but also of Rome's admiration for Egyptian civilization. In modern times, the obelisk has encouraged monuments around the world, serving as a lasting symbol of the ancient Egyptians' architectural prowess and spiritual depth. The lasting fascination with obelisks reflects not just their architectural grandeur but also their opulent symbolic meanings. As solar symbols, they encapsulate the ancient Egyptians' reverence for the sun and its life-giving power. As religious monuments, they embody the deep connection between the divine and the terrestrial, the sky and the earth. As embodiments of Ma'at, they stand as eternal reminders of the quest for harmony, order, and stability, both in the cosmos and in human society.

Essentially, the obelisk's significance in Egyptian symbolism is multifaceted, embodying the civilization's religious beliefs, cosmological views, and artistic achievements. These monumental stone pillars are not merely relics of a bygone era but powerful symbols of the ancient Egyptians' quest to understand and harness the divine forces that governed the world around them. Through the obelisk, they sought to bridge the earthly and the heavenly, ensuring the flow of divine blessings and affirming their place in the order of the cosmos.

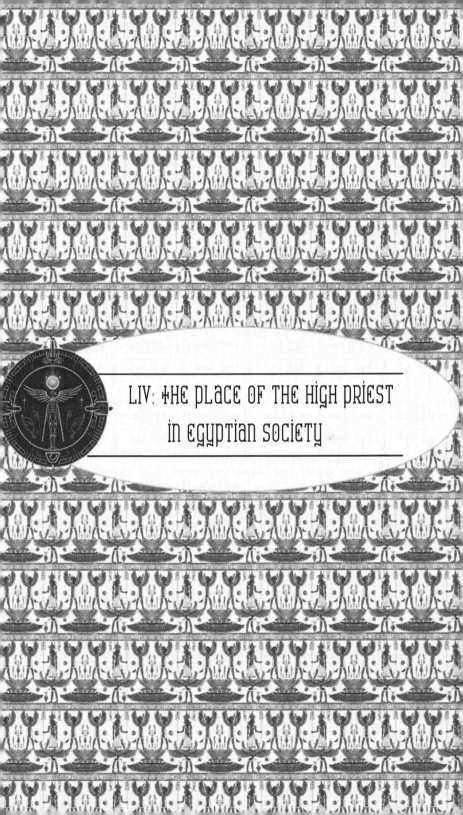

LIV: THE PLACE OF THE HIGH PRIEST IN EGYPTIAN SOCIETY

The place of the High Priest in ancient Egyptian society was necessary, encompassing religious, administrative, and political functions that placed them at the nexus of the civilization's spiritual and temporal worlds. As intermediaries between the gods and the people, High Priests were not just religious leaders but also key figures in the administration of temple estates and the broader economic life of Egypt. Their position required a deep knowledge of ritual practices, theology, and sacred texts, making them among the most educated and influential members of society.

Spiritual Leadership and Ritual Duties

The primary place of the High Priest was to act as the chief intermediary in the temple's interactions with the deity it was dedicated to. This involved overseeing the daily rituals, including the opening of the sanctuary at dawn, the offering of food, drink, and incense to the god's statue, and the performance of special ceremonies during religious festivals. These rituals were believed to sustain the gods and ensure their favor towards Egypt and its people. The High Priest, therefore, held a necessary place in maintaining Ma'at, the universal order, through these religious practices. In addition to daily temple rituals, High Priests were responsible for the organization and execution of major religious festivals, which often involved processions, music, and the public display of the god's statue. These events not just reinforced the bond between the deity and the community but also showcased the temple's wealth and the High Priest's power.

Administrative and Economic Responsibilities

The economic power of the temples in ancient Egypt was giant, with lands, workshops, and extensive personnel dedicated to the production of goods for the temple and the market. The High Priest was at the helm of this economic powerhouse, overseeing the administration of the temple's assets, including agricultural lands, storehouses, and artisan workshops. This place required a sophisticated understanding of economics and administration, as the temple's wealth needed to be managed to support its religious activities and contribute to the wider economy.

High Priests also held a key place in redistributing wealth within society through the temple's place in collecting and storing grain and other goods, which could be distributed to the needy in times of famine. This not just reinforced the temple's central place in society but also the High Priest's status as a benefactor of the people.

Political Influence

Given their control over giant temple estates and their place in key religious ceremonies, High Priests wielded significant political influence. They often served as advisors to the pharaoh and could be involved in state affairs, particularly those that intersected with religious matters. In periods of decentralization or political instability, High Priests could become the de facto rulers of their regions, commanding loyalty through their religious and economic power. The relationship between the pharaoh and the High Priests was complex, characterized by mutual dependence and occasional tension. While the pharaoh was respected as a god on earth, the High Priest's authority in religious matters gave him a unique status that could rival the pharaoh's, particularly in matters concerning the gods' will.

Education and the Preservation of Knowledge

High Priests were custodians of sacred knowledge, responsible for the education of the priesthood and the maintenance of the temple's library, which housed religious texts, astronomical records, and medical treatises. This place made them key figures in the preservation and transmission of Egypt's religious and scientific knowledge, contributing to the civilization's intellectual and spiritual heritage.

The place of the High Priest in ancient Egyptian society was multifaceted, reflecting the intertwined nature of religion, politics, and economics in the civilization. As spiritual leaders, they sustained the gods and maintained universal order through ritual practices. As administrators, they managed the temple's giant resources, playing a key place in the economic life of Egypt. As political figures, they wielded significant influence, serving as advisors to the pharaoh and occasionally acting as regional rulers. And as educators, they preserved and transmitted Egypt's sacred knowledge, ensuring the continuity of its religious traditions.

The High Priest was a central figure in ancient Egyptian society, embodying the civilization's spiritual aspirations and its practical achievements. Their heritage is a confirmation of the sophisticated religious and social systems that characterized ancient Egypt, highlighting the civilization's lasting fascination with the divine and its ingenious ways of integrating religious practice into the map of daily life.

LV: The Interpretation of Omens and Signs in Egyptian Rituals

The interpretation of omens and signs in ancient Egyptian rituals reflects the civilization's complex belief system, where the natural and supernatural worlds were intimately intertwined. The Egyptians believed that the gods communicated with them through various omens and signs, manifesting in the environment, dreams, and even through the behavior of animals. These communications were not random; instead, they were respected as deliberate messages from the divine, offering guidance, warnings, or affirmations to the living. The ability to correctly interpret these signs was a highly respected skill, often associated with priests, magicians, and oracles, who served as intermediaries between the gods and the people.

Omens in the Natural World

The ancient Egyptians saw the natural world as a source of divine messages, where phenomena like the flooding of the Nile, the movement of stars, and even the behavior of the Nile's creatures could be interpreted as signs from the gods. The annual inundation of the Nile was perhaps the most significant omen, with its timing, extent, and duration seen as indicators of the gods' favor or displeasure. A bountiful flood was a sign of divine blessing, promising a fruitful harvest, while a low flood could be interpreted as a warning of hard times ahead. Astronomical events, like eclipses and the heliacal rising of Sirius (the Dog Star), were also opulent with symbolic meaning. These events were carefully recorded and interpreted, guiding agricultural practices, religious festivals, and even the pharaoh's decisions. The appearance of certain stars or constellations could be read as omens for the best times to plant or harvest crops, or as signs heralding significant religious events.

Animal Behavior and Omens

Animals held a special place in Egyptian cosmology, with certain species respected as sacred and others seen as embodiments of deities. The behavior of these animals was closely observed for omens. For instance, the movement of the Apis bull, a living symbol of Ptah and later associated with Osiris, was carefully interpreted for messages about the future. Similarly, the behavior of cats, protected and respected for their association with Bastet, the goddess of home, fertility, and childbirth, could also be seen as portentous. Crocodiles, associated with the god Sobek, and ibises, linked to Thoth, were other examples of animals whose behaviors were scrutinized for divine messages. The presence of a crocodile near a town or a temple, or an ibis acting in an unusual manner, could be interpreted in multiple ways, depending on the context and the prevailing circumstances.

Dreams as Omens

Dreams were another necessary medium through which omens were received and interpreted. The ancient Egyptians believed that dreams could foretell the future, offer solutions to problems, or convey messages from the gods. The interpretation of dreams was a specialized skill, often performed by priests or individuals with the gift of insight. Significant dreams were recorded and analyzed, with their meanings deciphered based on a complex set of symbols and associations.

The Place of Divination

Divination was a formal means of interpreting omens and seeking guidance from the gods. Various methods were used, including the casting of lots, the examination of entrails, and the interpretation of water ripples. These practices allowed the Egyptians to make decisions, predict the outcome of events, and determine the will of the gods with greater certainty.

Omens in Rituals and State Affairs

The interpretation of omens held a necessary place in rituals and state affairs. Before embarking on military campaigns, constructing temples, or making significant political decisions, omens were sought and interpreted to ensure divine approval and success. Negative omens could lead to the postponement or cancellation of actions, reflecting the deep integration of omens into the decision-making processes of ancient Egyptian society. The interpretation of omens and signs in ancient Egyptian rituals stands for a fascinating convergence of religion, natural observation, and statecraft. It underscores the Egyptians' desire to live in harmony with the divine order, their respect for the natural world as a source of wisdom, and their belief in the enmeshment of all aspects of existence. Through the careful observation and interpretation of omens, ancient Egyptians sought to align their actions with the will of the gods, ensuring prosperity, protection, and the maintenance of Ma'at in both the natural and supernatural worlds.

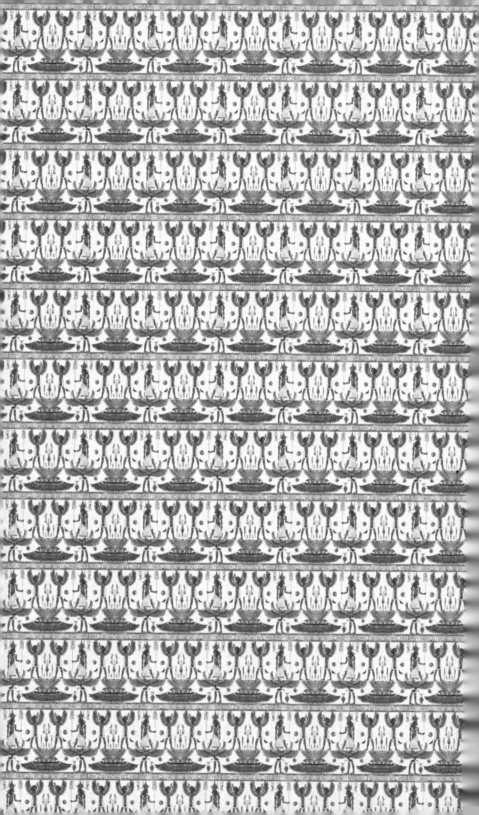

LVI: THE SYMBOLIC MEANING OF EGYPTIAN JEWELRY

The symbolic meaning of Egyptian jewelry transcends mere adornment, embodying the civilization's intricate belief systems, values, and cosmological views. Ancient Egyptians placed great significance on jewelry, not just for its beauty but also for its magical and protective properties. Jewelry pieces were crafted from a variety of materials, including gold, silver, precious stones, and colored glass, each chosen for its symbolic significance and inherent properties. The designs, motifs, and inscriptions found on these pieces were deeply grounded in Egyptian mythology, religion, and the pursuit of immortality, reflecting the civilization's sophisticated spiritual and philosophical outlook.

Materials and Symbolism

Gold, respected for its imperishable nature, was the most favored material in Egyptian jewelry, symbolizing the flesh of the gods, particularly that of the sun god Ra. Its incorruptibility and brilliance were associated with eternal life and the divine. Silver, though less common, represented the bones of the gods and was often used in combination with gold to evoke the duality of the divine essence. Semi-precious stones and colored glass were selected for their colors and properties, each imbued with specific meanings: lapis lazuli, symbolizing the night sky and the heavens, was linked to royalty and the gods; carnelian represented the blood of Isis and was believed to protect against harm; turquoise stood for joy and happiness; and amethyst was associated with healing and protection.

Protective Amulets

Jewelry in ancient Egypt often took the form of amulets and talismans, designed to protect the wearer in life and the afterlife. These items were believed to carry magical properties, with specific shapes and motifs invoking the protection of the gods. The Eye of Horus (Wedjat Eye), for instance, was a powerful symbol of protection, health, and restoration, representing the healed eye of Horus and offering protection against evil. The Scarab beetle, symbolizing rebirth and the rising sun, was another popular amulet, often inscribed with spells from the Book of the Dead to ensure resurrection and immortality.

Jewelry in Life and Death

Egyptian jewelry was worn by both the living and the dead. For the living, jewelry signified social status, protected against evil forces, and expressed religious devotion. The dead, however, were adorned with jewelry to prepare them for the afterlife, with amulets playing a necessary place in ensuring their safety and rebirth. Jewelry pieces were often placed strategically on the mummy, with heart scarabs placed over the heart to prevent it from testifying against the deceased during the judgment of the soul.

Symbolic Motifs and Designs

The designs and motifs used in Egyptian jewelry were opulent with symbolic meaning, often depicting deities, sacred animals, and symbols of power and protection. The Ankh, representing life and immortality, was a common motif, embodying the key to the afterlife. The Djed pillar, symbolizing stability and endurance, was another important symbol, often worn as an amulet or incorporated into jewelry designs to invoke the protection of Osiris. The use of these and other symbols in jewelry design served to communicate the wearer's beliefs, aspirations, and allegiance to specific deities.

Royal and Divine Jewelry

Jewelry also held a significant place in the divine and royal iconography of ancient Egypt. Deities were often depicted wearing elaborate collars, headdresses, and other ornaments, underscoring their divine status and powers. Pharaohs and queens, as divine representatives on earth, adorned themselves with luxurious jewelry to assert their authority, divine favor, and connection to the gods. The crowns, pectoral collars, and ceremonial regalia of the royalty were laden with symbolic motifs and inscriptions, designed to protect the wearer and affirm their place in maintaining universal order.

The symbolic meaning of Egyptian jewelry is a confirmation of the civilization's deep engagement with the divine, the natural world, and the afterlife. Through the careful selection of materials, the use of protective amulets, and the incorporation of meaningful motifs and designs, jewelry served as a potent expression of ancient Egyptian religious beliefs, social identity, and cosmological understanding. It was a means of invoking divine protection, affirming one's status and beliefs, and securing a place in the eternal afterlife. The opulent symbolism embodied in Egyptian jewelry continues to fascinate and encourage, offering insight into the complex relationship of art, religion, and society in ancient Egypt.

LVII: THE FESTIVAL OF THE VALLEY: HONORING THE DEAD

The Festival of the Valley, also known as the Beautiful Feast of the Valley, was one of ancient Egypt's most significant religious celebrations, deeply embedded in the civilization's rituals and symbolism concerning the dead and the afterlife. This festival, celebrated in Thebes (modern Luxor), exemplified the Egyptians' profound reverence for their ancestors, the enmeshment of life and death, and the cyclical nature of existence. It provided a structured occasion for the living to honor the dead, reaffirming the bonds between them and ensuring the deceased's wellness in the afterlife.

Origins and Historical Context

The Festival of the Valley began during the Middle Kingdom but gained prominence in the New Kingdom, a period marked by profound religious fervor and elaborate funerary practices. It was celebrated annually, coinciding with the flood season of the Nile, which symbolized renewal and fertility. The festival's timing underscored the Egyptians' belief in the regenerative powers of the Nile and its connection to the cycle of life, death, and rebirth.

Rituals and Celebrations

The festival centered around a procession of the god Amun's cult statue from Karnak to the West Bank of Thebes, where the royal necropolis and mortuary temples were located. This adventure mirrored the sun's daily passage across the sky and its nightly adventure through the underworld, reinforcing the universal significance of the event. Amun's barque, accompanied by a flotilla of boats carrying priests, dignitaries, and worshippers, was a spectacle of religious devotion, with music, singing, and the burning of incense enhancing the sacred atmosphere. Upon reaching the West Bank, the procession visited the tombs and mortuary temples, where rituals were performed to honor the deceased. Families of the dead participated in these rituals, bringing offerings of food, flowers, and libations to the tombs. These offerings were intended to sustain the ka (spirit) of the deceased, ensuring their continued wellness in the afterlife.

Symbolic Reconnection with the Dead

The Festival of the Valley served as a symbolic reconnection between the living and the dead, emphasizing the lasting bonds of family and community. The act of visiting the tombs, cleaning and decorating them, and presenting offerings was a manifestation of filial piety and respect for the ancestors. It mirrored the Egyptians' belief in the necessity of maintaining these bonds to ensure both the deceased's peaceful existence in the afterlife and the continued prosperity of the living.

The Place of the Community

While the festival had a strong familial component, it was also a community event that reinforced social cohesion and shared religious beliefs. The collective participation in the procession, rituals, and feasting fostered a sense of unity and shared identity among the inhabitants of Thebes. The festival underscored the community's place in upholding ma'at, the universal order, through the proper observance of religious rites and the veneration of the dead.

Reflections on Mortality and the Afterlife

The Festival of the Valley prompted reflections on mortality, the afterlife, and the cyclical nature of existence. By honoring the dead, the living engaged with their own mortality and the inevitability of death. However, the festival also affirmed the Egyptians' belief in the afterlife as a continuation of existence, where the dead lived on in a transformed state. The joyous celebrations, amidst tombs and mortuary temples, underscored the Egyptians' acceptance of death as a part of life and their optimism about the afterlife. The Festival of the Valley was a multifaceted event that encapsulated ancient Egypt's complex beliefs about death, the afterlife, and the cosmos. It was an occasion for honoring the dead, reaffirming familial and community bonds, and celebrating the regenerative powers of the Nile and the cycle of life. Through its rituals and celebrations, the festival expressed the Egyptians' reverence for the past, their engagement with the present, and their hopes for the future. It remains a piercing example of ancient Egypt's religious and cultural vitality, highlighting the civilization's profound engagement with the mysteries of existence and the lasting human desire to connect with the divine and the departed.

VIII: THE CONCEPT OF CHAOS AND ORDER IN EGYPTIAN MYTHOLOGY

The concept of chaos (Isfet) and order (Ma'at) is foundational in ancient Egyptian mythology, permeating their cosmology, rituals, and the very map of society. This dualistic notion not just shaped the Egyptians' worldview but also underscored their religious practices, governance, and daily life. Central to Egyptian thought was the belief that the universe emerged from a primordial state of chaos, and through the divine act of creation, order was established. This order, however, was not permanent; it required constant maintenance and renewal through the actions of the gods and the pharaoh, the divine representative on Earth.

The Primordial Chaos and the Emergence of Order

In the beginning, according to Egyptian mythology, there was Nun, the chaotic waters that represented the abyss of chaos before creation. From these waters emerged the benben, the primordial mound, upon which the god Atum (or Ra, in some traditions) stood. Through an act of self-creation or masturbation, Atum generated Shu (air) and Tefnut (moisture), who in turn begot Geb (earth) and Nut (sky), establishing the fundamental elements of the cosmos. This narrative illustrates the Egyptians' conception of the universe's emergence from chaos through divine action, resulting in the establishment of Ma'at, the order that sustains all aspects of existence.

Ma'at: The Principle of Universal Order

Ma'at, often personified as a goddess wearing an ostrich feather, represented truth, justice, harmony, and balance. It was the principle that sustained the gods, humans, and the cosmos itself, ensuring the regularity of the seasons, the flooding of the Nile, and the movements of the stars. Ma'at was both a universal principle and a moral one, guiding human actions and the laws of society. The pharaoh, as the guarantor of Ma'at, had the responsibility to uphold this order through governance, religious rituals, and personal conduct. The concept of Ma'at was so integral to Egyptian society that it permeated their art, literature, and judicial system, embodying the ideal state of existence toward which individuals and the state aspired.

Isfet: The Force of Chaos

Contrasting with Ma'at was Isfet, the principle of chaos, disorder, falsehood, and injustice. Isfet was not merely the absence of order but an active force that sought to return the cosmos to its primordial state of chaos. The struggle between order and chaos was a recurring theme in Egyptian mythology, exemplified

in the battles between Horus, the god of kingship and protector of Ma'at, and Seth, the god
associated with chaos, storms, and violence. This
universal struggle mirrored the daily challenges
faced by the Egyptians, both individually and
collectively, to maintain order in their lives and
society against the forces of disorder.

The Maintenance of Universal Order

The maintenance of Ma'at required the
participation of both the divine and the human
worlds. The gods, through their actions and in-
terventions, fought against the forces of chaos
and upheld the universal order. Ra's daily adventure across the sky in his solar barque, accompanied by other deities, was a continual reaffirmation of Ma'at, as he battled the serpent Apophis,
the embodiment of Isfet, to ensure the sun's rebirth each morning. On Earth, the pharaoh and
the priests performed rituals and offerings to the
gods to honor them and secure their favor,
thereby reinforcing Ma'at in the human world.
The citizens, in turn, were expected to live according to the principles of Ma'at, practicing
truth, justice, and harmony in their interactions
with others.

The Symbolism of Chaos and Order in Daily Life

The symbolism of chaos and order extended to every aspect of Egyptian life, all the way from the layout of their temples and cities, designed to reflect universal order, to the rites of passage that marked an individual's adventure through life. Funerary practices, in particular, were aimed at ensuring the deceased's transition from the chaos of death to the ordered existence of the afterlife, guided by spells and rituals that invoked Ma'at and protected against Isfet.

The concept of chaos and order in Egyptian mythology stands for a fundamental aspect of ancient Egyptian thought, reflecting their understanding of the universe, the divine, and the moral obligations of humanity. Through the perpetual struggle between Ma'at and Isfet, the Egyptians saw the cosmos as a dynamic system, constantly at risk but sustained through the actions of the gods and the adherence of humanity to the principles of order. This worldview not just provided a scaffolding for their religious beliefs and practices but also offered a guide for personal conduct and governance, emphasizing the importance of harmony, balance, and justice in achieving a well-ordered life and society.

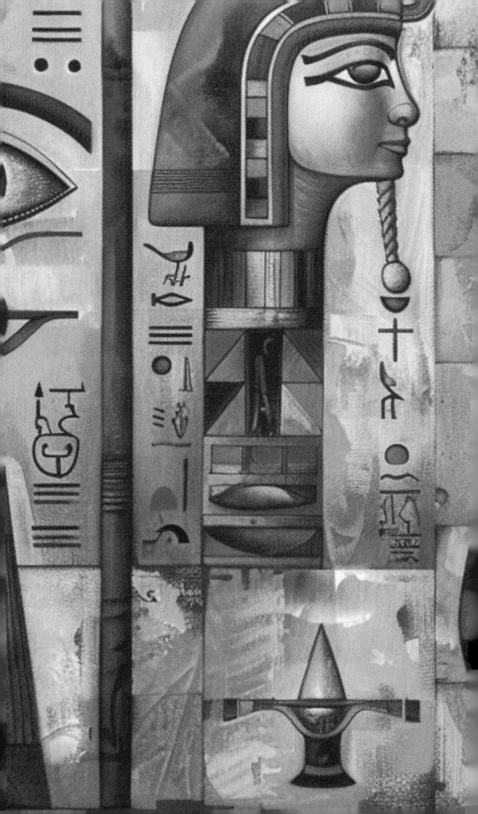

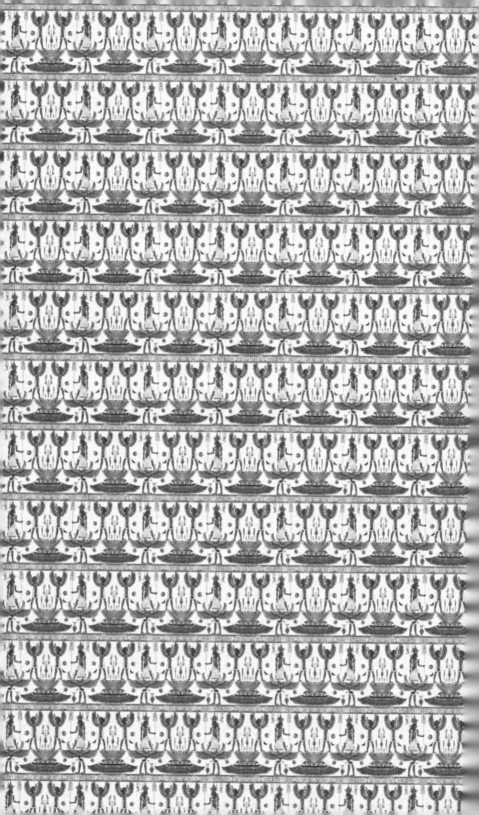

LIX: ꝉHE RELATIONSHIP BETWEEN EGYPTIAN ART AND RITUAL PRACTICE

The relationship between Egyptian art and ritual practice is a profound reflection of how deeply intercharted art was with the spiritual and ceremonial life of ancient Egypt. This symbiotic relationship underscores not just the Egyptians' aesthetic achievements but also their complex belief systems, where art served as a conduit to the divine, a means to immortalize and honor the dead, and a method to enact and symbolize ritual practices. Through careful craftsmanship, symbolic representation, and the integration of art into religious ceremonies, the ancient Egyptians created a visual language that communicated their cosmological views, values, and aspirations.

Art as a Medium for Divine Communication

Egyptian art was not merely decorative but was imbued with deep religious significance, serving as a medium for communication with the divine. Temples, the houses of the gods, were adorned with intricate reliefs, paintings, and statues that depicted the deities in various forms, engaging in acts of creation, granting boons to the pharaohs, and participating in sacred rituals. These artistic representations were not simply illustrative but were believed to hold the essence of the divine, making the gods present within the sacred spaces. The act of creating these images was itself a ritual, with artists and craftsmen undergoing purification rites before undertaking their work, ensuring that their creations were fit for divine habitation and worship.

Symbolism and Iconography in Ritual Contexts

The symbolism and iconography inherent in Egyptian art held a necessary place in ritual practice. Every image, color, and symbol was selected for its associative meanings and its ability to convey complex theological concepts and cosmological truths. For instance, the ankh symbolized life and was frequently depicted in the hands of gods, extending it towards the nostrils of the pharaoh, symbolizing the breath of life being conferred upon him. Similarly, the djed pillar, representing stability and endurance, was often incorporated into scenes depicting religious ceremonies, emphasizing the ritual's place in maintaining universal order.

Funerary Art and the Rituals of the Afterlife

Funerary art is perhaps the most striking example of the relationship between art and ritual in ancient Egypt. Tombs were adorned with paintings, reliefs, and objects designed to ensure the deceased's safe passage to the afterlife, provide protection against malevolent forces, and guarantee a continuation of life beyond death. The walls of burial chambers were inscribed with scenes from the Book of the Dead and other funerary texts, depicting the deceased's adventure through the underworld and their presentation before Osiris. These images served both as guides for the soul of the deceased and as magical protections, embodying the spells and incantations that would secure their resurrection and immortality.

The Place of Statuary

Statuary also held a significant place in Egyptian ritual practice. Statues of deities, the pharaoh, and private individuals were not merely representational but were believed to house the ka, or spirit, of the being they depicted. Offerings were made to these statues as part of daily temple rituals, treating them as living entities. In funerary contexts, statues served as eternal homes for the deceased's ka, ensuring their survival in the afterlife. The creation of these statues was governed by strict conventions and rituals, ensuring their effectiveness as vessels for the ka and their ability to function within the prescribed religious scaffolding.

Rituals of Creation and Consecration

The creation of art was itself ritualized, with specific prayers, spells, and ceremonies accompanying the crafting of religious and funerary objects. The "Opening of the Mouth" ceremony, performed on statues and funerary effigies, was a ritual of animation, transforming the object from a mere representation to a living embodiment of the divine or the deceased. This ritual illustrates the power attributed to art within the Egyptian religious paradigm, where objects could be imbued with life and agency through the appropriate rites.

The relationship between Egyptian art and ritual practice is indicative of a culture that perceived the visual arts as an essential element of the religious and ceremonial map of society. Through art, the ancient Egyptians sought to manifest the divine on earth, ensure the efficacy of their rituals, and secure their place in the afterlife. This integration of art and ritual underscores the Egyptians' belief in the power of images and symbols to influence the divine world, protect and sustain the living and the dead, and maintain the universal order upon which their civilization depended. Egyptian art, therefore, stands not just as a confirmation of the civilization's artistic achievements but also as a profound expression of its spiritual and ritualistic life.

Ancient Egyptian
Rituals and Symbolism

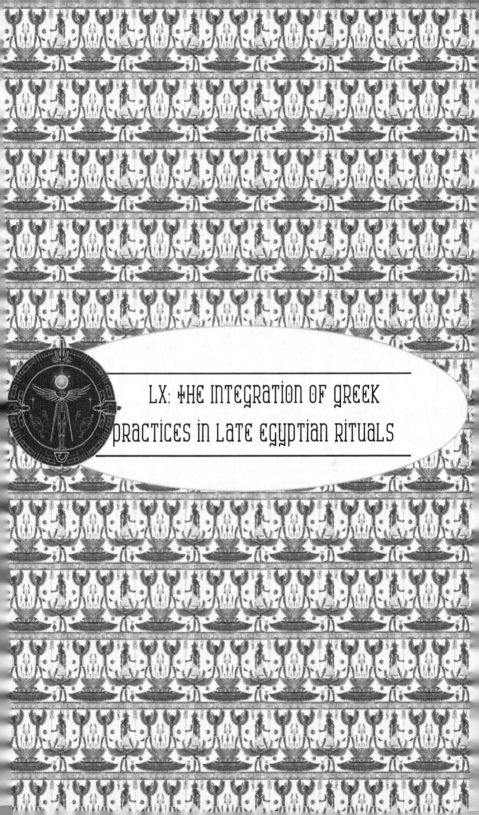

LX: The Integration of Greek Practices in Late Egyptian Rituals

The integration of Greek practices into late Egyptian rituals stands for a fascinating chapter in the history of ancient Egypt, a period marked by cultural exchanges and the blending of religious traditions. This phenomenon occurred predominantly during the Ptolemaic Dynasty, following the conquest of Egypt by Alexander the Great in 332 BCE, which led to the establishment of a Greek ruling class in Egypt that lasted until the Roman conquest in 30 BCE. The Ptolemaic period is characterized by a syncretic approach to religion, as Greek and Egyptian beliefs and practices intertwined, leading to the emergence of new deities, cults, and ritual practices that mirrored the fusion of these two opulent cultures.

Greek Influence on Egyptian Religion

The Greeks, upon their arrival in Egypt, showed a deep respect for the ancient Egyptian religion, recognizing the parallels between their gods and the Egyptian deities. This mutual recognition facilitated the integration of Greek practices into Egyptian rituals and vice versa. Greek rulers often portrayed themselves as pharaohs and participated in traditional Egyptian religious ceremonies, adopting Egyptian titles and incorporating themselves into the long lineage of Egyptian monarchs. This adoption and adaptation were strategic, aimed at legitimizing their rule and bridging the cultural divide between the Greek rulers and the Egyptian populace.

Syncretism and the Creation of New Deities

One of the most significant outcomes of the Greek presence in Egypt was the syncretism observed in the religious sphere, exemplified by the creation of Serapis. Serapis was a composite deity, conceived by Ptolemy I Soter to unite Greek and Egyptian worshippers under a common god. Serapis combined aspects of Osiris and Apis with attributes of Greek gods like Zeus, Dionysus, and Hades. The cult of Serapis quickly gained popularity, symbolizing the fusion of Greek and Egyptian religious traditions. The Serapeum in Alexandria, dedicated to Serapis, became a prominent religious and cultural center, attracting pilgrims and scholars from across the Mediterranean world.

Adaptation of Ritual Practices

The integration of Greek practices into Egyptian rituals can also be seen in the adaptation of traditional ceremonies to include Greek elements. Greek festivals and processions began to feature alongside traditional Egyptian religious celebrations, sometimes merging into hybrid events that mirrored the dual heritage of the Ptolemaic Kingdom. For example, the

Ptolemaic rulers introduced the festival of the Ptolemaia, which combined Greek athletic competitions with traditional Egyptian religious processions, celebrating the ruler's divine status and the prosperity of the kingdom.

Greek Contributions to Egyptian Temples

Greek influence extended to the architectural and artistic domains, with Greek-style temples and statuary erected alongside traditional Egyptian structures. These temples often housed cults dedicated to syncretic deities like Serapis and Isis, who was increasingly venerated in a form that merged her attributes with those of Greek goddesses like Demeter and Aphrodite. Greek inscriptions and imagery appeared in Egyptian temples, and vice versa, illustrating the deep cultural exchange between the two civilizations.

The Effect on Funerary Practices

Greek practices also influenced Egyptian funerary rituals, with the introduction of new burial customs and the adoption of Greek funerary art styles. Sarcophagi 'and tomb paintings began to exhibit Greek artistic influences, while still adhering to traditional Egyptian themes and iconography. The use of Greek inscriptions alongside hieroglyphs in tombs and on mummies' coffins further exemplifies the blending of these two cultures in the world of the afterlife.

The integration of Greek practices into late Egyptian rituals reflects the dynamic and syncretic nature of Ptolemaic Egypt, a period of cultural fusion and religious innovation. This blending of traditions resulted in an opulent atlas of beliefs and practices that expanded the religious territory of Egypt, introducing new deities, cults, and ceremonial practices that have enriched our understanding of ancient religious syncretism. The heritage of this period is a confirmation of the adaptability and inclusiveness of Egyptian religion, illustrating how deeply interconnected the experience of humanity of the sacred can be across different cultures and epochs.

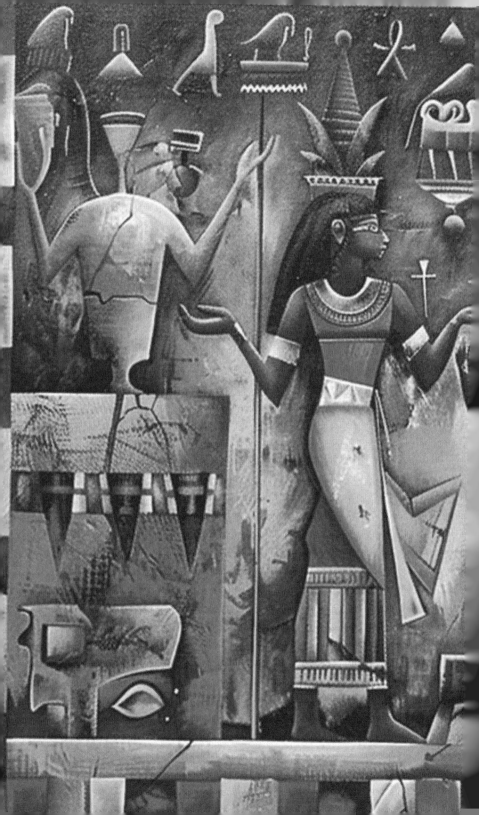

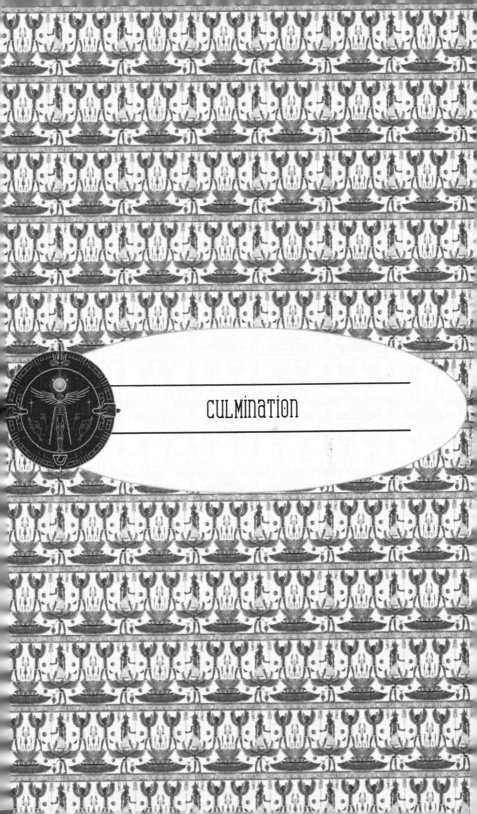

CULMINATION

And here we are at the end of our long boat ride down the Nile. The adventure of ancient Egyptian rituals and symbolism offers a profound adventure into one of humanity's oldest spiritual landscapes, revealing a world where every symbol, myth, and ritual practice was imbued with deep esoteric significance. This civilization's religious and philosophical system, with its intricate understanding of the cosmos, the divine, and the soul of humanity's adventure, provides an invaluable resource for esoteric religious studies. It opens avenues for understanding the perennial quest for meaning, the nature of the divine, and the intricate relationship between the material and the spiritual worlds. The themes addressed in the study of ancient Egyptian rituals and symbolism—ranging from the dynamics of chaos and order, the significance of life and the afterlife, to the power of sacred geometry and the place of the divine intermediary—vibe with core concerns of esoteric spirituality. These themes reflect a sophisticated theological and cosmological worldview that sees the universe as an interconnected whole, governed by divine laws and accessible to human understanding through symbolic language and ritual engagement.

The concept of Ma'at, embodying universal truth, justice, and balance, offers insights into the Egyptians' view of a morally ordered universe, where human actions contribute to the maintenance of universal harmony. This principle, along with the ritual practices aimed at sustaining the gods and ensuring the balance between the physical and spiritual worlds, underscores the active place of humanity in participating in the divine order. Such ideas echo in many esoteric traditions, which emphasize the cultivation of virtue, harmony, and spiritual insight as pathways to personal and universal transformation.

The detailed symbolism found in Egyptian art, architecture, and funerary practices provides an opulent atlas of metaphysical knowledge and esoteric wisdom. The use of symbols, like the ankh, the djed pillar, and the scarab, as well as the architectural alignments and sacred geometries of temples and pyramids, reveals a deep engagement with the mysteries of life, death, and the afterlife. These symbols and structures not just served religious and ceremonial purposes but also encoded profound spiritual teachings, offering keys to understanding the nature of the soul, the afterlife, and the process of spiritual regeneration.

The integration of Greek practices into late Egyptian rituals during the Ptolemaic period exemplifies the dynamic and syncretic nature of ancient Egyptian religion, highlighting the capacity of spiritual traditions to evolve and adapt over time. This period of cultural and religious fusion further enriches the esoteric heritage of ancient Egypt, demonstrating the enmeshment of the ancient world and the shared human quest for divine knowledge and understanding. The study of ancient Egyptian rituals and symbolism within esoteric religious studies provides invaluable insights into the spiritual aspirations, theological concepts, and cosmological visions of one of the world's oldest civilizations. It reveals a complex and nuanced spiritual tradition that continues to encourage and inform contemporary esoteric thought, offering eternal wisdom on reality's nature, the pursuit of harmony, and the quest for eternal life. Through a deep engagement with the opulent heritage of ancient Egyptian spirituality, modern seekers and scholars alike can uncover lasting truths about the cosmos, the divine, and the soul of humanity's place within the giant atlas of existence.

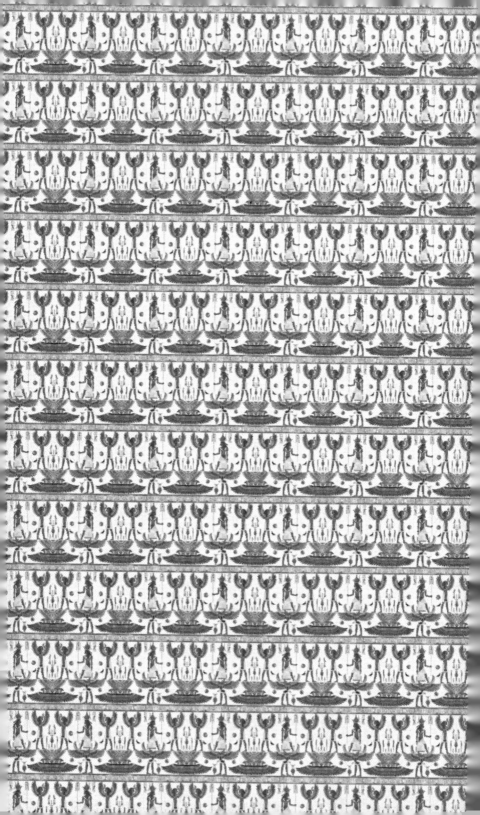

INDEX OF IMPORTANT TERMS

- **Akhenaten**: Pharaoh known for establishing a monotheistic worship centered around Aten.
- **Akhet**: The horizon symbol associated with the sun rising and setting.
- **Amulet**: Small objects worn for protection or to confer special powers, often depicting gods, symbols, or hieroglyphs.
- **Ankh**: Symbol representing life and immortality.
- **Anubis**: God of mummification and the afterlife, often depicted as a jackal or with a jackal's head.
- **Apis**: Sacred bull associated with Ptah, later integrated into the Osiris myth.
- **Aten**: Sun disk, worshiped as the sole deity in the monotheistic religion promoted by Akhenaten.
- **Atum**: Creator god who emerged from the primordial waters of Nun.
- **Ba**: Aspect of the soul represented as a human-headed bird, symbolizing personality or individuality.
- **Benben**: The primordial mound in Egyptian creation myths, also a type of obelisk.
- **Benben stone**: A pyramidal stone symbolizing the primeval mound upon which Atum stood.
- **Bes**: Dwarf deity associated with household protection, childbirth, and entertainment.
- **Book of Caverns**: A funerary text describing the sun god's adventure through the underworld.

- **Book of Gates**: A funerary text outlining the gates and worlds of the afterlife that the deceased must navigate.
- **Book of the Dead**: A collection of spells, prayers, and incantations intended to guide the deceased through the afterlife.
- **Cartouche**: An oval with a horizontal line at one end, encircling a royal name.
- **Cleopatra**: The last active ruler of the Ptolemaic Kingdom of Egypt.
- **Coffin Texts**: Middle Kingdom funerary spells inscribed on coffins to protect and guide the dead in the afterlife.
- **Decree of Canopus**: A stele with religious reforms and calendar adjustments.
- **Deshret**: The red crown of Lower Egypt.
- **Djed**: Symbol representing stability, associated with Osiris.
- **Djoser**: A pharaoh of the Third Dynasty, associated with the Step Pyramid.
- **Duat**: The Egyptian underworld or world of the dead.
- **Eye of Horus**: A symbol of protection, royal power, and good health.
- **Eye of Ra**: Protective symbol associated with the sun god Ra.
- **Feather of Ma'at**: Symbol of truth, balance, and universal order.
- **Field of Reeds**: The Egyptian paradise in the afterlife.
- **Geb**: God of the earth.

- **Hathor**: Goddess of love, beauty, music, and motherhood.
- **Heart Scarab**: Amulets placed over the heart of the mummified deceased to protect against the judgment in the afterlife.
- **Hedjet**: The white crown of Upper Egypt.
- **Heb Sed**: A rejuvenation festival for the pharaoh.
- **High Priest of Amun**: The chief priest in the temple of Amun at Thebes.
- **Hieroglyphs**: The writing system of ancient Egypt, consisting of pictorial symbols.
- **Horus**: Sky god, often depicted as a falcon; associated with kingship.
- **Imhotep**: Architect, priest, and later deified as a god of wisdom and medicine.
- **Isfet**: The concept of chaos, disorder, and falsehood.
- **Isis**: Goddess of magic, motherhood, and fertility.
- **Judgment of the Dead**: The trial in the afterlife where the heart is weighed against the feather of Ma'at.
- **Ka**: The spiritual double that resides in the body.
- **Karnak**: A major temple complex in Thebes dedicated to Amun.
- **Khepresh**: The blue crown, worn in battle.
- **Kiosk of Trajan**: A structure in the Philae temple complex from the Roman period.

- **Lector Priest**: A priest who read sacred texts during rituals.
- **Lotus**: Symbol of creation, rebirth, and the sun.
- **Luxor**: Site of the ancient city of Thebes, opulent in temples and monuments.
- **Ma'at**: The principle of truth, balance, and universal order.
- **Mastaba**: An early flat-roofed tomb structure.
- **Medjay**: Nubian desert scouts, later police and military in Egypt.
- **Memphis**: Ancient capital of Egypt, an important cultural and political center.
- **Merkhet**: Ancient timekeeping instrument.
- **Mummification**: The process of preserving the body for the afterlife.
- **Mut**: Mother goddess, wife of Amun.
- **Natron**: A salt used in the mummification process to dry out the body.
- **Necropolis**: Literally "city of the dead"; a large ancient cemetery.
- **Nefertiti**: Queen of Egypt and wife of Akhenaten, known for her beauty and power.
- **Nemes**: The striped headcloth worn by pharaohs.
- **Nome**: An administrative division of ancient Egypt.
- **Nun**: The primordial waters from which the world was created.
- **Obelisk**: A tall, four-sided, narrow tapering monument with a pyramidion on top.

- **Opet Festival**: A festival in Thebes celebrating the renewal of kingship.
- **Osiris**: God of the afterlife, death, life, and resurrection.
- **Ostracon**: A piece of pottery or stone used as a writing surface.
- **Per Ankh**: "House of Life"; an institution or library associated with a temple.
- **Per Nefer**: "Beautiful House"; a place where mummification was performed.
- **Papyrus**: A plant used to make a writing material of the same name.
- **Ptah**: God of craftsmen and architects.
- **Ptolemy**: Name of Greek rulers of Egypt after Alexander the Great's conquest.
- **Pschent**: The double crown of Upper and Lower Egypt.
- **Pyramid**: Monumental structure used as a royal tomb.
- **Pyramid Texts**: The oldest known religious texts, found in pyramids.
- **Ramesseum**: Memorial temple of Ramses II.
- **Ra**: Sun god and creator deity.
- **Rosetta Stone**: Key to deciphering Egyptian hieroglyph

s.
- Sarcophagus: Stone coffin, often inscribed or decorated.
- Scarab: Beetle symbolizing the sun, rebirth, and protection.

- **Sed Festival**: Ritual celebrating the pharaoh's continued rule and rejuvenation.
- **Sekhmet**: Lioness goddess associated with war and healing.
- **Serapis**: Hellenistic god combining aspects of Osiris and the Apis bull.
- **Serdab**: A sealed chamber in a tomb containing a statue of the deceased.
- **Seshat**: Goddess of writing and measurement.
- **Seth**: God of chaos, desert, and storms.
- **Shabti**: Funerary figurines intended to act as servants for the deceased in the afterlife.
- **Shu**: God of air and light.
- **Sistrum**: A musical instrument used in religious ceremonies.
- **Sobek**: Crocodile god associated with the Nile and military might.
- **Statuary**: Sculpture representing gods, pharaohs, or notable individuals, often used in religious contexts.
- **Taweret**: Hippopotamus goddess associated with childbirth and fertility.
- **Thoth**: God of writing, knowledge, and the moon.
- **Tutankhamun**: Pharaoh of the 18th dynasty, famous for his intact tomb.
- **Uraeus**: The rearing cobra symbolizing sovereignty and divine authority.
- **Valley of the Kings**: Burial site for New Kingdom pharaohs.

- **Valley of the Queens**: Burial site for queens and royal children.
- **Was**: A scepter symbolizing power and dominion.
- **Wab Priest**: A priest responsible for purification rituals.
- **Zep Tepi**: The "First Time" or primeval age when the gods ruled on earth.

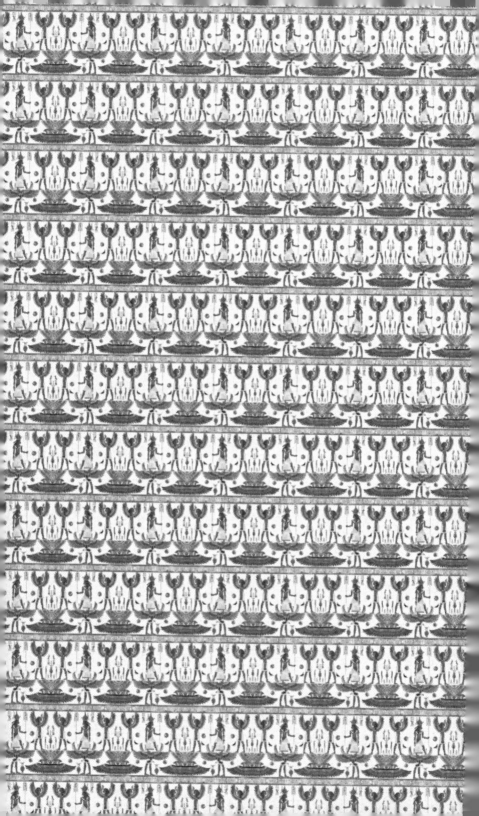

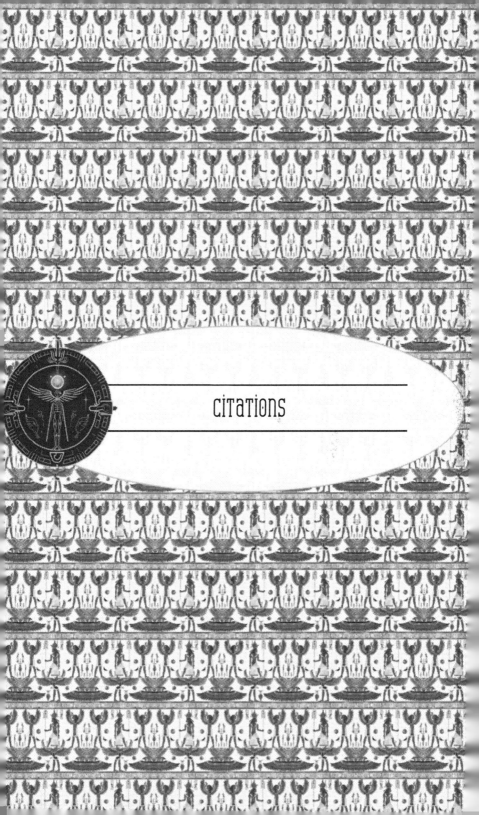

citations

Allen, J. P. (2005). The ancient Egyptian pyramid texts. Society of Biblical Literature.

Allen, J. P. (2014). Middle Egyptian: An introduction to the language and culture of hieroglyphs (3rd ed.). Cambridge University Press.

Allen, T. G. (1974). The book of the dead or going forth by day: Ideas of the ancient Egyptians concerning the hereafter as expressed in their own terms. University of Chicago Press.

Ancient History Encyclopedia. (n.d.) Ma'at. Retrieved from https://www.ancient.eu/Maat/Ancient History Encyclopedia. (n.d.) Ra.

Andrews, C. (1994). Amulets of ancient Egypt. University of Texas Press. (Explores how amulets relate to protection in the Duat)

Arnold, D. (1991). Building in Egypt: Pharaonic stone masonry. Oxford University Press.

Assmann, J. (2001). The search for God in ancient Egypt. Cornell University Press.

Assmann, J. (2003). Solar religion and kingship in the Old Kingdom. In Z. Hawass & J. Wegner (Eds.), Old Kingdom studies (pp. 47–60). American University in Cairo Press.

Assmann, J. (2005). Death and salvation in ancient Egypt. Cornell University Press.

Assmann, J. (2006). Ma'at: Gerechtigkeit und Unsterblichkeit im Alten Ägypten. C.H. Beck. (Note: This book is in German)

Badawy, A. (1968). A history of Egyptian architecture (Vol. 3). University of California Press.

Baines, J. (1991). Egyptian religion: Continuity and change in the latest centuries before the Roman conquest. In Civilizations of the Ancient Near East (pp. 1645–1661). Scribner and Sons.

Baines, J. (1991). Society, morality, and religious practice. In B. E. Shafer (Ed.), Religion in ancient Egypt: Gods, myths, and personal practice (pp. 123–200). Cornell University Press.

Baines, J. (1995). Kingship, definition of culture, and legitimation. In D. O'Connor & D. P. Silverman (Eds.), Ancient Egyptian kingship (pp. 3-47). Brill.

Baines, J., & Malek, J. (2000). Cultural atlas of Ancient Egypt. Checkmark Books.

Bárta, M. (2000). The evolution of Old Kingdom burial practices: Some aspects of social development. In M. Bárta, & J. Krejčí (Eds.), Abusir and Saqqara in the Year 2000 (pp. 41-58). Academy of Sciences of the Czech Republic, Oriental Institute.

Bell, L. (1985). The nature of the Egyptian priesthood: Part I. The place of the priest in Egyptian society. Bulletin de l'Institut Français d'Archéologie Orientale, 85, 43–78.

Bell, L. (1985). The temple complex as cosmos. In Luxor Temple and the cult of the royal ka. Journal of Near Eastern Studies, 44(4), 251–267. British Museum. (n.d.) The adventure through the underworld.

The British Museum. (n.d.). Death and afterlife in ancient Egypt.

Burkert, W. (1985). Greek religion. Harvard University Press. (Examines connections between Greek and Near Eastern, including Egyptian, religion)

Collier, M., & Manley, B. (1998). How to read Egyptian hieroglyphs: A step-by-step guide to teach yourself British Museum Press.

Davies, W. V. (1987). Egyptian Hieroglyphs. University of California Press.

David, R. (2002). Religion and magic in ancient Egypt. Penguin Books.

Eyre, C.J. (1984). Crime and punishment in ancient Egypt. The Journal of Egyptian Archaeology, 70, 100-111.

Faulkner, R. O. (1962). A concise dictionary of Middle Egyptian. Griffith Institute.

Faulkner, R. O. (1973). The ancient Egyptian coffin texts (Vol. 1-3). Aris & Phillips.

Finnestad, R. (1985). Image of the world and symbol of the creator: On the cosmological-symbolic parallelism in the ancient Egyptian temple. In E. Hornung, & O. Keel (Eds.), Studien zu altägyptischen Lebensvorstellungen (pp. 52–83). Otto Harrassowitz.

Frankfurter, D. (1998) Religion in Roman Egypt: Assimilation and resistance. Princeton University Press.

Gillam, R. (1995). Priestesses of Hathor: Their function, decline and disappearance. Journal of the American Research Center in Egypt, 32, 211–237.

Goldwasser, O. (2002). An Egyptian scribe from the early New Kingdom: Reflections on a religious text. Revue d'Égyptologie, 53, 95–125.

Gorton, T. (2016). Egyptian influences on Roman Religion. In E. Frood, & W. J. T. Mirecki (Eds.), Time and religion in Ancient Egypt (pp. 297–318). Cambridge Scholars Publishing.

The Griffith Institute, Oxford. (n.d.). Hieroglyphs.

Griffiths, J. G. (1960). Aspects of Egyptian religious iconography. Journal of Near Eastern Studies, 19(2), 76–82.

Hornung, E. (1996). Conceptions of God in ancient Egypt: The One and the Many (D. Lorton, Trans.). Cornell University Press.

Hornung, E. (1999). The Egyptian Duat, the Western horizon, and the Hereafter. Zeitschrift für Ägyptische Sprache und Altertumskunde (Journal of Egyptian Language and Archaeology), 126(2), 119-134.

Hornung, E. (1999). The Secret Lore of Egypt: Its Effect on the West. Cornell University Press.

Hornung, E., & Lorton, D. (1999). The ancient Egyptian books of the afterlife (D. Lorton, Trans.). Cornell University Press.

Ikram, S., & Dodson, A. (1998). The mummy in ancient Egypt: Equipping the dead for eternity. Thames & Hudson.

Karenga, M. (2004). Maat, the moral ideal in ancient Egypt: A study in classical African ethics. Routledge.

Kemp, B. (2006). Ancient Egypt: Anatomy of a civilization. Routledge.

Lehner, M. (1997). The complete pyramids. Thames & Hudson. (Focuses on pyramid development, which ties into funerary practices)

Lichtheim, M. (1976). Ancient Egyptian literature, Vol. II: The New Kingdom. University of California Press. (Contains translations of texts discussing Ma'at)

Luiselli, M. M. (2021). Writing and rewriting sacred landscapes at Karnak in the 22nd Dynasty. Journal of Egyptian Archaeology, 107(1), 43-64.

Metropolitan Museum of Art. (n.d.). The pharaoh's place in daily temple rituals. Retrieved from https://www.metmuseum.org/toah/hd/phar/hd_phar.htm

The Metropolitan Museum of Art's Heilbrunn Timeline of Art History. Egyptian Art: Religion and Ritual.

The Metropolitan Museum of Art. (n.d.) Ancient Egyptian Writing.

Pinch, G. (1994). Passing through the Netherworld: the meaning and play of images in Egyptian funerary texts. Journal of the Royal Anthropological Institute, 129-151.

Pinch, G. (2002). Offering to Re and his rising. In P. Kousoulis (Ed.), Ancient Egyptian religion and funerary beliefs (pp. 83–93). Archaeopress.

Pinch, G. (2004). Handbook of Egyptian mythology. ABC-CLIO.

Pinch, G. (2004). Magic in Ancient Egypt. University of Texas Press.

Redford, D. B. (Ed.). (2002). The Oxford essential guide to Egyptian mythology. Berkley Books.

Ritner, R. K. (1993). Egypt under Roman rule: the heritage of ancient Egypt. In J. H. Johnson

(Ed.), The Cambridge companion to Egypt (pp. 99–119). Cambridge University Press.

Smith, M. (2009). Evolution of the embalming ritual in ancient Egypt. In S. Ikram, & B. Kaiser (Eds.), Annales du Service des Antiquités de l'Égypte: Hommages à Fayza Haikal (pp. 321-329). Supreme Council of Antiquities Press.

Spencer, A.J. (1982). Death in ancient Egypt. Penguin Books.

Swillam, A. A. (2014). Symbolism in ancient Egyptian architecture. International Journal of Research in Humanities and Social Studies, 1(5).

Taylor, J. (2001). Death and the afterlife in ancient Egypt. University of Chicago Press.

Taylor, J. H. (2000). Spatial aspects of the adventure to the afterlife in Old Kingdom Egypt. In Bárta, M. & Krejčí, J. (Eds.), Abusir and Saqqara in the Year 2000 (Proceedings of Conference, Prague, 2000) (pp. 485–495). Prague: Academy of Sciences of the Czech Republic, Oriental Institute.

Taylor, J. H. (2010). Adventure through the afterlife: Ancient Egyptian Book of the Dead. British Museum Press.

Teeter, E. (2011). Religion and ritual in ancient Egypt. Cambridge University Press.

Tobin, V.A. (1989). Theological principles and the king's duties in Ma'at. Zeitschrift für Ägyptische Sprache und Altertumskunde (Journal of Egyptian Language and Archaeology), 116, 11-21.

University College London. (n.d.). Digital Egypt for Universities: Kingship.

University College London. (n.d.). Digital Egypt for Universities: Ma'at.

University College London. (n.d.). Digital Egypt for Universities: Temple architecture.

University College London. (n.d.) Digital Egypt for Universities: The Netherworld and its denizens.

University of Cambridge, Fitzwilliam Museum. (n.d.). Ancient Egyptian Funerals.

University of Chicago, Oriental Institute: (n.d.) Ancient Egyptian Religion and its Influence.

Vernus, P. (1990). Studies on the temple of Khonsu, Vol. 1: Scenes of king Herihor in the court- problems of religious iconography and

Egyptian kingship in the Ramesside Period. Bulletin - Institut Francais d'Archeologie Orientale, 90, 262-263.

Wilkinson, R. H. (2000). The complete temples of ancient Egypt. Thames & Hudson.

Wilkinson, R. H. (2003). The complete gods and goddesses of ancient Egypt. Thames & Hudson.

ESOTERIC RELIGIOUS STUDIES SERIES

Ω

OMEGA

Dear student of the **Esoteric Religious Studies Series**, we express our deepest gratitude for departing on this enlightening adventure. Having dived into the worlds of esoteric *wisdom*, may you carry the flame of knowledge within your being. May the insights gained and the revelations experienced guide your path as you get into the atlas of life. May the *wisdom* you have acquired permeate every aspect of your existence, nurturing your spirit and triggering your actions. May you carry on to seek truth, look favorably towards growth, and walk the path of *wisdom* with grace and compassion. May your life be a confirmation of the transformative power of esoteric knowledge.

If you have enjoyed the words of this book, please consider leaving a review in the marketplace you found it so that its content can enrich the lives of others.

OTHER BOOKS IN THIS SERIES

A WORLD OF ESOTERIC THOUGHT

ESOTERIC RELIGIOUS STUDIES SERIES

For more esoteric religious studies, please visit
Mythological Center by scanning the following QR code:

or by visiting https://mythological.center online.

ISBN: 9798882626401

Made in the USA
Columbia, SC
15 December 2024

49480889R00274